"Mark Fisher was a brilliant public speaker. He found new connections between music, psychoanalysis and politics. His lectures opened the world, making it available not just for critique but for comradeship."

— **JODI DEAN**, AUTHOR OF *COMRADE: AN ESSAY ON POLITICAL BELONGING*

"Mark Fisher has proven to be one of the most influential thinkers of our time. These lectures are a fantastic resource for those of us interested in consciousness, counterculture, and communism. To read them is to remember, once again, Mark's relentless appetite for the emancipation of desire from capital."

— **HELEN HESTER**, AUTHOR OF *XENOFEMINISM*

"Mark's unparalleled ability to infuse ideas with life comes across beautifully in these lectures. Throughout his work, he never stopped believing in and working towards an escape from capitalism — and this series of talks finds Mark weaving his way through working-class history, countercultural libidinal movements, and high theory in an unwavering effort to find just such an escape."

— **NICK SRNICEK**, AUTHOR OF *PLATFORM CAPITALISM*

"How can the libidinal infrastructure of capitalism be confronted and reconfigured for communism? These lectures, intimate and exploratory, don't have all the answers — more vital than that, they show the necessity of this wrenching question in our catastrophic times."

— **NICHOLAS THOBURN**, AUTHOR OF *ANTI-BOOK: ON THE ART AND POLITICS OF RADICAL PUBLISHING*

POSTCAPITALIST DESIRE

POSTCAPITALIST DESIRE:
THE FINAL LECTURES

Mark Fisher

Edited and with
an Introduction
by Matt Colquhoun

Published by Repeater Books

An imprint of Watkins Media Ltd

Unit 11 Shepperton House

88-93 Shepperton Road

London

N1 3DF

UK

www.repeaterbooks.com

A Repeater Books hardback original 2021

2

CONTENTS

Introduction:
No More Miserable Monday Mornings
By Matt Colquhoun

Atrocity Exhibition

In the introduction to his unfinished book, *Acid Communism*, the late Mark Fisher — famous for his love of post-punk, jungle, and a range of contemporary pop-experimentalists — surprised friends and fans alike by writing positively about the counterculture of the 1960s and 1970s.

Fisher had previously been scathing about the legacy of the counterculture. He had once declared on his *k-punk* blog, for instance, that "hippie was fundamentally a middle class male phenomenon" defined by a "hedonic infantilism".[1] For him, the hippie's characteristic sloppiness, "ill-fitting clothes, unkempt appearance and Fuzzed-out psychedelic fascist drug talk, displayed a disdain for sensuality".[2] For Mark Fisher, there was no greater crime. The hippies, as if trapped in an *Invasion of the Body Snatchers*-type scenario of their own devising, were guilty of passively and mindlessly giving in to the pleasure principle, and the "price of such 'happiness' — a state of cored-out, cheery Pod people affectlessness — [was the] sacrifice of all autonomy".[3]

As far as Fisher was concerned, to self-induce a stoned stupor, chemically or otherwise, was to do capitalism's work for it, as if driven by a Freudian "repetition compulsion" to artificially implement capitalism's cognitive capture from within, demonstrating the human organism's "marked ... tendency to seek out and identify itself with parasites that debilitate but never quite destroy it".[4] Instead, on his *k-punk* blog in particular, Fisher offered another path. This path did not require the superficial primitivism of showering less and smoking more, nor was it akin to a New Age overreliance on positive but hollow affirmations. If we are to take our psychedelic dream of emancipation seriously, and if it is to have any contemporary relevance whatsoever, we have to realise that nothing can be achieved by getting off your head on drugs. This was not a moral point, however, but an acutely political one. The point was, instead, "to get out *through* your head", through the application of a "psychedelic reason", "auto-effect[ing] your brain into a state of ecstasy".[5]

Fisher furnished his alternative with the seventeenth-century philosophy of Baruch Spinoza, where this "psychedelic reason" lies in wait, ready to be uncovered. "Spinoza is the prince of philosophers; really, the only one you need", he writes.[6] Before Deleuze and Guattari, Freud and Lacan, it was Spinoza who held the key to exorcising that parasitic demon of modernity, the capitalist ego, from one's mind. He notes that Spinoza "took for granted what would later become the first principle of Marx's thought — that it was more important to change the world than to interpret it". Spinoza attempted to do this by constructing a reflexive ethical project that was "effectively psychoanalysis three hundred years early".[7] Fisher continues:

> Vernacular psychology has it that emotions are irreducibly mysterious, too fuzzy and indistinct to analyse beyond a certain point. Spinoza, on the other

hand, maintains that happiness is a matter of *emotional engineering*: a precise science which can be learned and practiced ... In tune with popular wisdom, Spinoza is clear that what brings wellbeing to one entity will [be] poison to another. The first and most overriding drive of any entity, Spinoza says, is its will to persist in its own being. When an entity starts to act against its own best interests, to destroy itself — as, sadly, Spinoza observes, humans are wont to do — it has been taken over by external forces. To be free and happy entails exorcising these invaders and acting in accordance with reason.[8]

In this sense, Fisher's blogospheric rallying cry was to argue that we already possess everything that we need to escape the confines of capitalist realism — that ideological straitjacket that keeps us compliant and unimaginative; the external invader constricting our minds, bodies, and the self-realisation of our being today. Drugs like acid or ecstasy might loosen up the mind to a certain degree, but they neglect the other, more lucidly existential parts of human subjectivity (our capacity to reason, our political agency), leaving them to rot and atrophy. In this sense, the problem with drugs, Fisher argues, is that they "are like an escape kit without an instruction manual".[9] "Taking MDMA is like improving [Microsoft] Windows: no matter how much tinkering $ Bill [Gates] does, MS Windows will always be shit because it is built on top of the rickety structure of DOS".[10] The drugs, then, are all too temporary — "using ecstasy will always fuck up in the end because [the] Human OS [Operating System] has not been taken out and dismantled".[11] As fun as they may be, in the grand scheme of things, and as the old song goes, *the drugs don't work, they just make things worse...*

However, when the hippies "rose from their supine

hedono-haze to assume power", Fisher continues — addressing the aesthetic ubiquity and cultural power of the counterculture that has lingered long past the movement's political usefulness — "they brought their contempt for sensuality with them".[12] Culturally speaking, the shadow of this moment is long. With the new sensuality of post-punk eventually defeated, Fisher connects the virulence of this "anti-sensual sensibility" to the cultural yuppies of the 1990s, epitomised by the Young British Artists, alongside the adjacent rise to power of Britpop's "laddishness".

It is hard to deny the prevalence of the counterculture's negative trajectory when framed in this way. Whilst at first it seems like there is little more than a similar predilection for round teashade sunglasses connecting the Beatles' John Lennon to Oasis's Liam Gallagher, for instance, in fact the counterculture's cul-de-sac of passivity — or, as Fisher puts it, its "hey man, it's all about the *mind*!" sensibility — was as much the driving force behind the "bleary, blurry, beery, leery, lairy" vibe of Britpop hedonism as it was for the acid tests of the bohemian unwashed.[13]

This is apparent as soon as we cast an eye over the acid mundanity captured in two songs — the Beatles' "Lucy in the Sky with Diamonds" (1967) and Oasis's "Champagne Supernova" (1995). Thirty years apart, from two (politically) distinct worlds, the bond of a psychedelic melancholia nonetheless binds them together. The same hauntological and melancholic transference can be seen in John Lennon and Yoko Ono's 1969 performative sit-in, "Bed-Ins for Peace", the rotten husk of which re-emerged from the funereal white cube of the Tate Gallery in the form of Tracey Emin's 1998 work "My Bed".

This superficial regurgitation of Sixties concerns under the melancholy of Nineties capitalism resembles the *fin de siècle* decadence of the previous century — a nightmarish and fumbling autopsy of a long-dead dream, albeit devoid of any of its proto-modernist self-awareness. Britpop, in this sense, was truly an atrocity exhibition, curating a fashion-show procession of neoliberal spectres and zombies, now haunting and stalking the psyche.

The Abstract Ecstasy of Psychedelic Reason

It is fair to say that nothing from this period of Fisher's blogging days — a particularly productive August in 2004 — constitutes "putting it lightly"; his critiques are barbed and often wholly negative. So how did *this* Mark Fisher transform into the Fisher of *Acid Communism*? Despite this unflattering appraisal from the mid-2000s, it seemed that Fisher later softened his opinion on the counterculture as a whole. And yet, despite appearances, this transformation was not so extreme. Fisher instead took it upon himself to move beyond his barbed critiques and work towards the construction of a positive political project — a project that still had his Spinozist "psychedelic reason" at its heart.

It seems that, in the process of constructing such a project, Fisher had begun to newly appreciate the political potentials of the counterculture's best cultural and aesthetic offerings — at least in their original socio-political context. These potentials were not to be found in the surrealist abstractions of a bourgeois Pink Floyd concert, repurposed nostalgically and apolitically for today. Instead, they were to be found explicitly in the cultural artefacts that built new bridges between class consciousness and psychedelic consciousness, between class consciousness and group consciousness, but which were smothered or abandoned before their time.[14]

For instance, in the introduction to *Acid Communism*, Fisher champions the Kinks' "Sunny Afternoon" and the

Beatles' "I'm Only Sleeping" as two tracks, both released in 1966, that were able to apprehend

> the anxiety-dream toil of everyday life from a perspective that floated alongside, above or beyond it: whether it was the busy street glimpsed from the high window of a late sleeper, whose bed becomes a gently idling rowing boat; the fog and frost of a Monday morning abjured from a sunny Sunday afternoon that does not need to end; or the urgencies of business airily disdained from the eyrie of a meandering aristocratic pile, now occupied by working-class dreamers who will never clock on again.[15]

There was more to this political provocation than the average BBC Radio 4 listener's dream of a quiet Sunday that never ends. More generally, Fisher was interested — and had always been interested — in the ways that radical political messages could be smuggled into collective consciousness through popular culture. He was also intrigued by the ways that pop culture could not only entice us with its infectious euphoria but also push past capitalism's co-option of the pleasure principle into something deeper, something altogether unconscious, and bring it kicking and screaming to the surface.

A number of questions nonetheless remain. Most importantly, Mark sought to ask where these potentials went, and why. It was obvious that, as he would later put it, the establishment feared nothing more than the working class becoming hippies — but why was this? What was it in the counterculture that threatened the establishment so much that a burgeoning neoliberal order saw it as necessary to implement a hostile takeover of a new collective consciousness? And might the renewed manifestation of some of these thwarted potentials still threaten the capitalist-realist establishment today?

These questions constitute a view of psychedelia that still needs to be affirmed. It is the dormant *function* of psychedelia, in this sense, rather than its familiar aesthetic form, that remains relevant to us in the present moment: the way the word itself, all aesthetic associations aside, connotes the manifestation of what is deep within the mind, not simply on its surface. An irregular conjunction of the modern English prefix "psyche" and the more blatant Greek root *"dēlos"* — meaning "manifest" or "reveal" — the psychedelic is that which manifests what is in the mind, echoing Marx's Spinozist adage, once again, that we must not settle for interpreting the world but instead strive to change it. This is not to set interpretation and manifestation in opposition, however — rather, the former must always strive to become the latter.

A new psychedelic culture is required, then, that will inform politics anew, but it may not look like we expect it to. Indeed, we should be vigilant against anything that appears too familiar. We might even argue that the aesthetic connotations of psychedelia today are to be rejected outright. As Fisher once wrote on Surrealism, one of countercultural psychedelia's clearest antecedents: "Like punk, Surrealism is dead as soon as it is reduced to an aesthetic style. It comes unlive again when it is instantiated as a delirial program (just as punk comes unlive when it is effectuated as an anti-authoritarian, acephalic contagion-network)".[16]

This is why the counterculture should be handled with care. In spite of, or perhaps because of, its contemporary romanticisation, it seems to have been the last time that a cultural revolution came close to effectuating a political one. Culture has nonetheless continued to develop apace, but politics has been sluggish to catch up. Nevertheless, there is still a great deal to be excited about, despite the state of the contemporary political establishment. As Fisher concludes in the introduction to *Acid Communism*: "Of course, we know that the revolution did not happen. But the material conditions for such a revolution are more in place in the twenty-first century than they were in 1977".[17] Rather than simply celebrating the potentials of the counterculture, Fisher had serious questions to ask about why it failed, and how we might learn from those lessons today. He continues:

> What has shifted beyond all recognition since then is the existential and emotional atmosphere. Populations are resigned to the sadness of work, even as they are told that automation is making their jobs disappear. We must regain the optimism of that Seventies moment, just as we must carefully analyse all the machineries that capital deployed to convert confidence into dejection. Understanding how this process of consciousness-deflation worked is the first step to reversing it.[18]

The essay ends on a cliffhanger, and this call to understand the process fades away, seemingly without a road map. Following Fisher's death in January 2017, the assumption has been that the particulars of *Acid Communism* were lost with their author. And yet, there remain plenty of breadcrumbs out in the world for the curious reader to consider. Perhaps the best thing to do is apply Fisher's advertised strategy to his own thinking: understanding how the project of *Acid Communism* emerged is the first step to reconstructing it.

Such a strategy requires a lot less speculation than one might first assume. Along with a disparate collection of essays, spanning the length of his career as a writer and critic, that reflect many of the themes and subjects he was expected to explore, there is also the structure of Fisher's final postgraduate lecture series, "Postcapitalist Desire", which he devised for the academic year of 2016/17 at Goldsmiths, University of London.

New Year, New You

The dawn of the academic year 2016/17 brought about a number of changes to the Visual Cultures department at Goldsmiths. This was true for everyone, but particularly Mark Fisher and Kodwo Eshun. Prior to that year, the pair had co-convened a postgraduate Master of Arts degree in Aural & Visual Cultures — a course which, in short, asked the question: "How do we think about the relation of sound and image in the era of ubiquitous media?" However, following a number of administrative changes within the university, this course — along with a handful of other, relatively small Masters courses — was to be subsumed into a pre-existing and now conglomerated MA course in Contemporary Art Theory.

These changes could have been taken as a loss for Fisher and Eshun, but they instead took the opportunity to try something new, leaving behind the focus of Aural & Visual Cultures to develop two separate modules that reflected their present interests. Whilst Eshun devised the "Geopoetics" seminar — a fifteen-week (very) close reading of Reza Negarestani's notoriously difficult 2008 work of theory-fiction, *Cyclonopedia*[19] — Fisher began "Postcapitalist Desire", a seminar in which he would explore the nefarious and entangled relationship between desire and capitalism, and the extent to which the former can both help and restrict us in our attempts to escape from the latter. It could also be seen as an attempt to workshop his next book: the now familiar work-in-progress, given the tentative title of *Acid Communism*.

The course took its name from an essay Fisher had previously published in 2012, exploring "the relation of desire to politics in a post-Fordist context".[20] Taking seriously a much ridiculed comment made by Conservative politician Louise Mensch on British television about the apparent hypocrisy of Occupy protesters in 2010 — protesters who decried capitalism whilst standing in line at Starbucks, tweeting about politics from their iPhones — Fisher argued that Mensch's position nonetheless warrants a serious response. This was to suggest that, whilst Mensch's cynicism was superficial, the implications of her critique remained deeply troubling. To what extent is our desire for postcapitalism always-already captured and neutralised by capitalism itself? How are we supposed to combat the "intensification of desire for consumer goods, funded by credit"?[21] Should we even try? For Fisher, the response to this problem cannot be, as Mensch suggests, a reactionary striving for a pre-capitalist primitivism; the "libidinal attractions of consumer capitalism", he suggests, need "to be met with a counterlibidio, not simply an anti-libidinal dampening".[22]

Fisher goes on to demonstrate this need through a close engagement with the "anti-Marxist" writings of his controversial former lecturer, Nick Land — in particular, Land's essay "Machinic Desire". Here Land argues, in his quintessential Nineties cyberpunk mode, for a kind of becoming-replicant, a becoming-immanent with the forces of capitalism. For Land, it is no longer "plausible that the relation between capital and desire is either external or supported by immanent contradiction, even if a few comical ascetics continue to assert that libidinal involvement with the commodity can be transcended by critical reason". Here, capital "is not an essence but a tendency".[23] Like the Lacanian death drive that asserts the innate nihilism of human existence to be a striving to return to the pre-oedipal calm of the womb, Land argues that capitalism persists today because cyberspace is "already under our skin", and to retreat from it is to retreat into some nonexistent pre-capitalist imaginary.[24] We have as much chance of escaping capitalism as we do of crawling back inside our mothers. As such, to attempt to separate our desires from capitalism is to stick a chest spreader in the still-kicking subject of modernity; the application of reason to such an innately irrational endeavour isn't good enough.

Despite Land's disavowal of the application of reason placing their projects in apparent opposition to one another, and as nightmarish as the modern Left more generally may find Land's appraisals, for Fisher the Left would nonetheless be remiss to ignore them.

The ways in which we can counter or ethically account for these critiques, by implementing a counterlibido to capitalist desire — a *post*capitalist desire — was to be the driving force behind Fisher's lecture series. For example, in the first lecture, he renewed this line of questioning, beginning once again with Mensch's provocation whilst also addressing some of his personal response's — that is, some of his *Acid Communism*'s — still unresolved tensions. However, before he and his students could look to a counter-libidinal future, just as he had forewarned his readers in the *Acid Communism* introduction, it was necessary that they first ascertained why any previous counterlibido had failed to effectuate and materialise real societal change.

The first few lectures of the course attempted to answer these questions through a variety of readings, from the densely theoretical to the journalistic and pop-historical. In the second lecture, for instance, addressing the perhaps surprising influence of Freudian psychoanalysis on the emerging counterculture, Fisher takes two contrasting views of the period: one from Frankfurt School philosopher Herbert Marcuse in 1955, the other from feminist essayist and music critic Ellen Willis in 1981. Taken together, they provide an insight into the period from a moment immediately prior to the counterculture's emergence, as well as a damning, posthumous account of its eventual failure.

It is an unnerving contrast. Marcuse's text remains as invigorating as it was over sixty years ago, but Willis's critiques also reverberate profoundly with our present. As Fisher wrote in a 2013 essay for *e-flux*:

> The Sixties counterculture might now have been reduced to a series of 'iconic' — overfamiliar, endlessly circulated, dehistoricized — aesthetic relics, stripped of political content, but Willis's work stands as a painful reminder of leftist failure. As Willis makes clear in her introduction to [her 1981 book] *Beginning to See the Light*, she frequently found herself at odds with what she experienced as the authoritarianism and statism of mainstream socialism. While the music she listened to spoke of freedom, socialism seemed to be about centralization and state control. The story of how the counterculture was co-opted by the neoliberal Right is now a familiar one, but the other side of this narrative is the Left's incapacity to transform itself in the face of the new forms of desire to which the counterculture gave voice.[25]

This critique could also be found in other examples of Fisher's writings from around this time: 2013 was also the year that he published his now infamous essay, "Exiting the Vampire Castle", for instance. What Willis had described from the dark side of the 1970s, Fisher saw continuing to undermine the hopes and dreams of the twenty-first-century left.

From the rift that emerged between the trade unions and the counterculture in America in the early 1970s to British Deputy Prime Minister John Prescott's 1997 declaration that "we're all middle class now", the latter half of the twentieth century was defined, in Fisher's mind at least, by the disarticulation of class from almost all cultural and political discourses. In the twenty-first century, however, class was making a comeback. From the rise of grime to mainstream popularity in the early 2000s to the publication of Owen Jones' 2011 book *Chavs*, a new class consciousness was emerging in Britain, presenting itself in many different forms. Unfortunately, this class consciousness still struggled to perforate what Fisher had referred to as a "febrile McCarthyite atmosphere fermented by the moralising left".[26]

Fisher's tone in "Exiting the Vampire Castle" was one of fury and impatience, disappointment and frustration. It was, after all, an exit — but only from social media. The response to the essay, from some quarters at least, could make the more casual interlocutor think that Fisher had turned his back on all that the Left held dear. It could be said that this was Fisher's critique from the other side also. In disarticulating class from the identitarian struggles of the day, capitalism no longer appeared to be the enemy. We were, instead, all too prone to impotently turning on one another.

At the time, this critique of the political landscape seemed to be wholly negative, populated as it was by a vampiric cast of energy-sucking trolls who used social media, and Twitter especially, to wholly deflate any emerging political group consciousness. Echoing the various descriptions of Grey Vampires that had peppered his *k-punk* blog — comment box marauders who "don't feed on energy directly, they feed on *obstructing projects*"[27] — Fisher deplored the complacent identitarian milieu of social media that seemed determined to undermine the most exciting pop cultural shift in decades. Although many rejected Fisher's appraisal outright, it was later vindicated in the years of the Brexit referendum and Jeremy Corbyn's leadership of the Labour Party — with the latter, in particular, constituting a potential reformation of left-wing politics in Britain: one that was as consistently undermined from within as it was from without.

The damage incurred by this political auto-immune disease, in all its guises, has been substantial — to class consciousness above all else. "Class consciousness is fragile and fleeting", Fisher argued, but the best way to combat this is to retain it as a topic of conversation. He continues: "The petit bourgeoisie which dominates the academy and the culture industry has all kinds of subtle deflections and preemptions which prevent the topic even coming up, and then, if it does come up, they make one think it is a terrible impertinence, a breach of etiquette, to raise it".[28] This indignation is as persistent as ever. However, the very fact that class consciousness must be persistently undermined gives us a sense of its nascent political power. Unfortunately, with Fisher's "Vampire Castle" going viral throughout the Anglosphere, igniting the social media outrage machine that he sought to critique, many wrote Fisher off entirely for committing the very cardinal sin he was hoping to call attention to: separating class consciousness from a consciousness of gender, race, or any other minoritarian category of self-identification. The reality of his position, as he would later take great care to emphasise, was quite to the contrary.

Consciousness Raising

Fisher later refined the argument he had made so polemically in "Exiting the Vampire Castle" by transforming his negative critique into a positive project of consciousness-raising. It was this same project that Fisher turned to in the third lecture of his "Postcapitalist Desire" course.

Becoming popular during the second-wave feminist movement of the 1960s and 1970s, "consciousness raising" was the name given to a practice of collective discussion that highlighted the inequalities under which people collectively lived. This was a necessary process because, as Fisher argued in his "Postcapitalist Desire" lectures, consciousness of one's material existence is, despite itself, not immediately self-evident. Instead, consciousness of one's place within a structure of inequality — be that capitalism, patriarchy or white supremacy — must be constructed; it is never given. The best way to construct such a consciousness is with the participation of others who share a similar material existence.

Writing for the political organisation Plan C about the psychedelic potentials still left to be extracted from a group practice like consciousness raising, Fisher explains:

To have one's consciousness raised is not merely to become aware of facts of which one was previously ignorant: it is instead to have one's whole relationship to the world shifted. The consciousness in question is not a consciousness of an already-existing state of affairs. Rather, consciousness-raising is productive. It creates a new subject — a *we* that is both the agent of struggle and what is struggled for. At the same time, consciousness-raising intervenes in the 'object', the world itself, which is now no longer apprehended as some static opacity, the nature of which is already decided, but as something that can be transformed. This transformation requires knowledge; it will not come about through spontaneity, voluntarism, the experiencing of ruptural events, or by virtue of marginality alone.[29]

In the present, whilst there are "agents of struggle" everywhere, what is struggled for is disparate and unclear. It even seems to be the case that certain modes of political consciousness, seized by capitalism itself, have been used precisely to fragment solidarity rather than create it. As individuals squabble over who has the most privilege on Twitter, for instance, turning on each other, the true enemy — capitalism itself — is left completely off the hook. It was Fisher's hope that these newly raised and yet fragmented forms of consciousness, proliferating under so-called "identity politics", could still find common ground that included a previously disarticulated class consciousness — a collective consciousness that builds an articulated awareness of minority struggles in order to better grasp the totality of the system at large: capitalism. This was necessary so that the left could produce what Fisher had once called, in his 2009 book *Capitalist Realism*, the "required subject — a collective subject".[30] Over the near-decade that followed the publication of his surprise bestseller, Fisher would further develop this concept of a collective subjectivity, coming to prefer the term "group consciousness".

Returning to his essay for Plan C, it was here that Fisher most successively elaborated on the need to extend the idea of consciousness beyond the individual. He writes:

Since consciousness-raising has been used by all kinds of subjugated groups, it would perhaps be better to talk now of subjugated group consciousness rather than (just) class consciousness ... Subjugated group consciousness is first of all a consciousness of the (cultural, political, existential) machineries which produce subjugation — the machineries which normalize the dominant group and create a sense of inferiority in the subjugated. But, secondly, it is also a consciousness of the potency of the subjugated group — a potency that depends upon this very raised state of consciousness.[31]

Unfortunately, in the years that followed the bruising reception of his "Exiting the Vampire Castle", this subjugated group consciousness kept on deflating. The Corbyn era of the Labour Party at first seemed to promise a revival, but the debacle of Brexit pricked any hope of this emerging consciousness coming to dominate. Whilst Fisher did not live to see the new lows to which Brexit would drag this consciousness, he nonetheless continued to highlight the incursions wrought upon it prior to that moment, in the hope that — just as Owen Jones had done in 2011 — shining a light on the right example at the right time might just wake the nation from its neoliberal stupor.

In 2014, for instance, Fisher turned to the controversial documentary series *Benefits Street*, which followed the lives of the residents of James Turner Street in Birmingham — a street that was supposedly home to more social welfare-dependent households than anywhere else in Britain. Writing for *New Humanist* magazine, Fisher argued that the programme, by its very nature, implied a default "bourgeois gaze, which judges working-class participants as lacking, by comparison with the middle class". "Moreover", Fisher continues, "this lack is understood in heavily moralised terms; it isn't to be explained by the working class's lack of resources or opportunities, but by a deficit in will and effort".[32]

In this sense, *Benefits Street* was a programme that portrayed an even more pernicious mutation within the ever-evolving nature of capitalist realism. Not only was capitalism deemed by the "realists" to be the only game in town, but the gaze of its central phantasmatic subject, the evergreen "middle class", was now taken to be the default subject position available as well. Whereas Fisher may have rejected the Nineties announcement that "we are all middle class now", our television screens continue to announce this reality silently and without fanfare nonetheless. The message, though implicit, is familiar: *there is no alternative.*[33]

Hang on Tight and Spit on Me

The enforcement of the middle class as a default subjective position would be skewered by Fisher in his final "Postcapitalist Desire" lecture before the Christmas break. Here, the fact that the working class might possibly find enjoyment in their own oppression becomes a challenge as darkly humorous as it is viscerally disenchanting. (The challenges put forth by Fisher's former lecturer, Nick Land, echo ominously here once again.)

Reading aloud from Jean-François Lyotard's viciously difficult 1974 book, *Libidinal Economy*, Fisher relishes the work's most polemical passages, as Lyotard seems to prophesy the patronising gaze cast upon James Turner Street, putting the producers on blast, who "dare not say the only important thing there is to say, that one can enjoy swallowing the shit of capital, its materials, its metal bars, its polystyrene, its books, its sausage pâtés, swallowing tonnes of it till you burst".[34] As far as Lyotard is concerned:

the English unemployed did not become workers to survive, they — hang on tight and spit on me — enjoyed the hysterical, masochistic, whatever exhaustion it was of hanging on in the mines, in the foundries, in the factories, in hell, they enjoyed it, enjoyed the mad destruction of their organic body which was indeed imposed upon them, they enjoyed the decomposition of their personal identity, the identity that the peasant tradition had constructed for them, enjoyed the dissolution of their families and villages, and enjoyed the new monstrous anonymity of the suburbs and the pubs in the morning and evening.[35]

Fisher had long taken Lyotard's charge, in all its dark humour, deadly seriously. In his 2010 essay "Terminator Versus Avatar", for instance, he updates Lyotard's provocation for the twenty-first century:

Hands up who wants to give up their anonymous suburbs and pubs and return to the organic mud of the peasantry. Hands up, that is to say, all those who really want to return to pre-capitalist territorialities, families and villages. Hands up, furthermore, those who really believe that these desires for a restored organic wholeness are extrinsic to late capitalist culture, rather than in fully incorporated components of the capitalist libidinal infrastructure.[36]

The working class of the twenty-first century are as entangled in their subordinated desire / desire for subordination as they were in the twentieth. But this apparent paradox of sadomasochistic desires is not without its uses. As Fisher continues: "Not far beneath Lyotard's 'desire-drunk yes', lies the No of hatred, anger and frustration: no satisfaction, no fun, no future. These are the resources of negativity that I believe the left must make contact with again".[37]

The left at large may not be ready for this at present — and Fisher himself may have softened his lust for negativity in the years to follow — but, just as the developing counterculture repeatedly foreshadowed the political sea-changes of the era, Lyotard's provocations find themselves encapsulated in much contemporary music and culture. Indeed, what is a *counter*culture if not a cultural hegemony recast in negative?

Whilst there are many examples to choose from in our present moment, this fire may find its most obvious spiritual successor in the Sleaford Mods, whose music oozes a fury in which economic and sexual frustration coalesce in a manner Lyotard first controversially put to work in his deeply transgressive theory of libidinal economy. On their 2008 track "Jobseeker", for instance, vocalist Jason Williamson hangs on tight and spits on you through the speakers, rehearsing a kind of spiteful inner monologue: what he wishes he could say to the superficially sympathetic bureaucrats at the job centre:

"So, Mr. Williamson, what have you done to find gainful employment since your last signing on date?" Fuck all! I've been sat around the house wanking. And I want to know why you don't serve coffee here. My signing on time is supposed to be ten past eleven. It's now twelve o'clock. And some of you smelly bastards need executing. ... "Mr. Williamson your employment history looks quite impressive. I'm looking at three managerial positions you previously held with quite reputable companies. Isn't this something you'd like to go back to?" Nah, I'd just end up robbing the fucking place. You've got a till full of twenties staring at you all day. I'm hardly going to bank it?[38]

The jobseeker rejects the moralised figure of the downtrodden and out of luck. It is the inverse of a figure like Daniel Blake, as seen in Ken Loach's critically acclaimed 2016 film *I, Daniel Blake*. Rather than raising consciousness through sympathy, depicting, through a fiction, the abject reality of the British welfare state, Williamson instead raises consciousness through bloody-mindedness, bottling the shame of class subordination and weaponizing it. This is not to say the Sleaford Mods' rejection of a Ken Loach image is a *rejection* of that form of political consciousness; it simply offers up an inverse image of proletarian subjectivity: ejected from the system and loving it. "Jobseeker" reinvigorates Lyotard's "desire-drunk yes", in this sense, affirming the fact that this uneasy subjugation is what makes the working class a threat to the system itself. *Fuck your middle-class propriety! I've got desires to pursue...*

Fisher's psychedelic reason still has a role to play here. The implication is that the "stay in bed, float upstream" anti-work ethic of the Beatles in the Sixties is more within reach for today's working class than it has ever been before. What was good enough for John and Yoko is certainly good enough for the jobseeker. Isn't it all the better the bed-in takes place in a flat in Grantham rather than a private suite at the Hilton Hotel?

Reflecting on the present accessibility of this potent affectivity in a review of two Sleaford Mods releases for *The Wire* magazine in 2014, Fisher writes that the sort of discontent Williamson gives voice to "is everywhere in the UK now but for the most part it's privatised: blunted by alcohol and antidepressants, or directed into impotent comment box spite and empty social media outrage".[39] But it is nonetheless "underscored by a class consciousness painfully aware that there is nothing which could transform disaffection into political action".[40] Many questions remain: "who will make contact with the anger and frustration that Williamson articulates? Who can convert this bad affect into a new political project?"[41] Who will seize this chemically-blunted disaffection and let it loose on the establishment?

This disaffection is, in a sense, only kindling to a wider movement. Is it doomed to impotence if the fire doesn't catch on the imagination of the demographic it gives voice to? Speaking about Lyotard with his students in late 2016, Fisher similarly admires the philosopher's "glorious hemmed in quality", but wonders if Lyotard's barbed rant is "a display of the glorious kind of autonomy and sufficiency of the text itself, or its impotence or uselessness?" These are the questions that continue to haunt culture today — and, if they haunt culture, they will inevitably haunt politics. Unless the strengths of the latter emerge from the former, we may find ourselves stuck in the same negative feedback loop.

Accelerate the Process

Fisher's "Postcapitalist Desire" lectures, much like the introduction to his *Acid Communism*, present themselves as an attempt to route around this capture. They ask, what is required of us if we truly want to push beyond capitalism? The suggestion that emerges from the fifth lecture of this series is that we must accelerate beyond the pleasure principle, beyond our culture of retrospection and pastiche, beyond the persistent disarticulation of group consciousness, beyond capitalist realism. In this sense, Fisher is attempting to describe to his students, from the ground up, a new praxis for a left-accelerationism.

Accelerationism is mentioned frequently throughout the lecture series — Fisher even goes so far as to claim the discourse surrounding the term to be "probably the biggest influence on the course" — but, from the vantage point of 2020, its appearance warrants some further context.

Accelerationism is much maligned today. Having garnered a (perhaps fatal) popular association with the far-right — with the term most repulsively appearing in the 2019 manifesto of Australian white supremacist and mass murderer Brenton Tarrant — the popular understanding of this philosophy's aims today is that capitalism (or the "status quo" more generally) is some barely functioning, unsustainable mess of contradictions; therefore, we should accelerate the mechanisms of capitalism (or the "status quo") towards their inevitable doom. This position is even more loosely (but frequently) translated as "things have to get worse before they can get better". However, as the philosopher Pete Wolfendale noted in 2015, "this is not a position that *anyone has ever held*".[42] In truth, the accelerationist position was a *critique* of the way that things are *only* getting worse. Crises, whether they be crises of capitalism or of protest — such as the financial crash of 2007/08 and the Occupy movement that followed it — no longer produce change; negativity destroys the old but no longer produces the new.

It was with this in mind that accelerationism — a term coined by Benjamin Noys in his 2010 critique of post-May 1968 Continental philosophy, *The Persistence of the Negative*[43] — was later seized upon by Mark Fisher and, perversely, affirmed. Noys' book was, by and large, a critique of how Continental philosophy was obsessed with affirming the negative. Fisher, in deftly trollish fashion, then affirmed Noys' negative critique. In hindsight, this may have been a mistake on Fisher's part but, for better or for worse, the name stuck, straddling a bizarre confluence of competing positions.

Fisher arguably usurped the term to demonstrate that Noys' seemingly benevolent position, looking down on this entanglement of negations and affirmations, was a fallacy. Whereas Noys attempted to untangle the mess, Fisher affirmed all sides, as if Noys' project was itself a reification of the negative — extending the very problematic it hoped to critique. Fisher was nonetheless attuned to the ways that this negative feedback loop of affirmations and negations was the primary cause of the hauntological "stuckness" of the twenty-first century. Indeed, the online discourse surrounding accelerationism had emerged explicitly from the financial crash of 2007/08, following which the Left and its protest movements seemed wholly incapable of effectuating real change. Whereas Noys was concerned about the extent to which a philosophical negativity had persisted, Fisher was concerned about how this negativity was now politically in crisis. Its presence was not a concern, but its impotence was. His accelerationist writings sought to establish a practical strategy for how this crisis might be overcome.[44]

Accelerationism, then, as hauntology's hyperactive cousin, was seen by Fisher and others as an analysis of the ever-increasing speed of technological progression under capitalism which sought to understand how this speed was affecting human cultural production and the production of subjectivity.[45] These accelerationist writers observed that, whilst capitalism continues to develop at exponentially greater speeds, we as the contemporary subjects of capitalism cannot keep up with the system we find ourselves enclosed within. As a result, culture stalls and causes drag on the system itself, which responds by pacifying our desires through superficial means and leads us to languish at the end of history. The Continental philosophers that Noys critiqued may have been incapable of preventing this acutely postmodern condition, but, for Fisher, to blame them for its ascendency was useless. No one else had gotten so close, philosophically speaking at least, to stalling our enclosure in what Fisher later described as our "frenzied stasis".

Nevertheless, it is from Noys' initial argument that most critiques of accelerationism now emerge. He had defined the theory under his critical eye as harbouring the belief that "if capitalism generates its own forces of dissolution then the necessity is to radicalise capitalism itself: the worse the better".[46] It was this that he referred to as Continental philosophy's accelerationist tendency; it is a tendency that the far-right have used to justify the encouragement of a race war. When Pete Wolfendale later argued that no one has ever held this position, he was attempting to clarify that accelerationism, in its newly affirmed mode, "is not about accelerating the contradictions of capitalism *in any sense*. Whatever is being accelerated, and there are severe and significant disagreements about this, it is not contradictions, and whatever transition this acceleration aims towards, it is not societal collapse".[47] By now, however, these objections to the accelerationist cliché too often fall on deaf ears. The reduction of Noys' critique of Continental philosophy has been affirmed in the worst sense and, at the level of popular discourse at least, it has won out.

The Becoming of History

Considering the other materials discussed in the "Postcapitalist Desire" lectures, we could argue that, for Fisher, what must be accelerated is the process of history. We might recall, for instance, Francis Fukuyama's famous

1992 text, *The End of History and the Last Man*, in which he announces not an end to things happening *as such*, but instead the ultimate ideological victory of capitalism — the by-product of which is the utter reification of history and our present hauntological stasis.

This issue lies in the background of Fisher's third lecture, in which he turns to *History and Class Consciousness*, the 1923 text by Hungarian philosopher György Lukács. Whilst Fisher focuses on the latter half of the work's title, Lukács nonetheless differentiates between an unending process of consciousness-raising and an immediately given — that is, superficial and fixed — self-consciousness of one's place within history. After all, we all know that history is written by the victors. For Lukács, capitalism's reification of history is one of the central strategies it has for cementing its position. He writes:

> Reification is, then, the necessary, immediate reality of every person living in capitalist society. It can be overcome only by *constant and constantly renewed efforts to disrupt the reified structure of existence by concretely relating to the concretely manifested contradictions of the total development, by becoming conscious of the immanent meanings of these contradictions for the total development.*[48]

Many self-identified accelerationists believe that the exacerbation of contradictions is the aim of the game. Not so. As Lukács makes clear, we must understand contradictions in their totality if we are to act differently. This argument, again, foreshadows Fisher's psychedelic reason. We must remember, Lukács writes, that history is mutable; it is not, as had been theorised since Hegel, "an insuperable barrier to a rationalist theory of knowledge."[49]

For Lukács, this is to say that human history is distinct from natural history. Our history is ideologically affected by our position in the present; geological history — foregoing presently contentious debates around the so-called "anthropocene" — is not. The events of human history — our wars, our elections, our culture — are not fossils embedded within the earth's geological strata — although capitalism certainly implores us to think this is the case.[50] On the contrary, history is not that which lies behind us in the past but rather that which occurs here with us in the present. History is the story of our own becoming, and in order to maintain that position, history must engage in its own process of becoming as well. Lukács writes: "It is only in history, in the historical process, in the uninterrupted outpouring of what is qualitatively new that the requisite paradigmatic order can be found in the realm of things."[51] History only happens, he argues, when things change. And who has the true capacity to change things? Only the proletariat. History, he writes — that is, *true* history — is "*the history of the unceasing overthrow of the objective forms that shape the life of man*"[52]; history is "the product (albeit the unconscious one) of man's own activity ... the succession of those processes in which the forms taken by this activity and the relations of man to himself (to nature, to other men) are overthrown."[53]

The problem in our presently postmodern moment, however, is accounting for the extent to which the working class, broadly speaking, *likes* history reified, *enjoys* the certainty of its narrative and its placing of our very being in legible stasis. It is this charge that concerns Lyotard in particular, as a figure who looms large in both Noys' critique and Fisher's affirmation of accelerationism.

To return to Wolfendale's article on the topic, he explains that, in mapping out some of the maligned theory's central philosophical antecedents, Lyotard's "attempt to combine Marxism and psychoanalysis has many problems ... but it does problematise the notions of desire and alienation in important ways."[54] What Lyotard argues, according to Wolfendale, anticipating Louise Mensch's cynical critique by over thirty years (and rejecting it), is that "there is no pure, authentic, or natural pre-capitalist form of life to return to", and so we must not "disavow the forms of living and desire that have been produced under capitalism, simply because of this fact of their genesis".[55] However, where we go from here remains a lively field for debate; what the nature of a postcapitalist society will be remains to be seen. Predicting the split that would later define accelerationist discourses online in the mid-2010s, Wolfendale writes that our speculation on this matter

> can descend into a perverse celebration of capitalism's destructive and oppressive tendencies (I'm looking at you, Lyotard), but it can equally become a call for greater self-consciousness regarding how we construct our desires and ourselves (here's looking at you, Foucault), an honest appraisal that refuses to be trapped within the nostalgic false-consciousness that seeps unbidden into so much leftist discourse.[56]

Here, Fisher's psychedelic reason once again rears its head, with accelerationism — as an admittedly broad church — contending precisely with the ways in which a reason under siege from the irreality of capitalism modernity can still give rise — as Spinoza declared — to actually-existing human freedom.

For Lukács, what is necessary seems clear. When accelerationists argue that "the only way out is through", they mean that the only way out is forwards; forwards in time and in history. There is no going back into the reified past. To attempt to do so is to accept the fate that the ideologues of capitalism want for us. As little agreement as there may be amongst other accelerationist factions, the process to be accelerated, in a Lukácsian sense, is history.

What Would Mark Fisher Do?

Unfortunately, the promise of this thought's further development was tragically interrupted. Following the Christmas break of 2016, Fisher's lecture series would not resume in the New Year. As a result, his final lecture on Lyotard is bittersweet. Little is resolved, but, following our engagement with these five lectures alone, we may nonetheless find ourselves in possession of a new knowledge — and, indeed, a new consciousness — regarding the circumstances in which we live and, in many ways, have always lived.

The sixth lecture in the series was scheduled to consider the autonomist movement in Italy in the late Seventies. In particular, Fisher asked his students to read a chapter from Nicholas Thoburn's 2003 book *Deleuze, Marx and Politics*. Although Fisher intended to focus specifically on the book's fifth chapter — on the politics of the refusal of work — it is nonetheless interesting to consider the fact that Thoburn's text is similarly concerned with the unrealised plans of a great thinker.

Before his death in 1995, Gilles Deleuze had announced that his final book would be called *The Grandeur of Marx*. It remains an intriguing title, not least because Deleuze's seemingly unorthodox Marxism has dogged the political reception of his work for many scholars. But, as Thoburn writes, this unfulfilled promise of a final work on Marx "leaves a fitting openness to [Deleuze's] corpus and an intriguing question."[57]

How was this philosopher of difference and complexity — for whom resonance rather than explication was the basis of philosophical engagement — to compose the 'greatness' of Marx? What kind of relations would Deleuze construct between himself and Marx, and what new lines of force would emerge? Engaging with this question and showing its importance, Éric Alliez [argues]: 'It can be realized therefore just how regrettable it is that Deleuze was not able to write the work he planned as his last...' But this is not an unproductive regret. For, as Alliez proposes, the missing book can mobilize new relations with Deleuze's work. Its very absence can induce an engagement with the 'virtual Marx' which traverses Deleuze's texts...[58]

The spectre of *Acid Communism* looms productively over Fisher's thought in much the same way. It is for this reason that these lectures have been gathered together and published in the present volume, with each discussion functioning as a bountiful toolbox to be put to endless use by the curious, provoking an engagement with the 'virtual communism' that Fisher had in mind. It was certainly not Fisher's intention to publish his thoughts in a form such as this, however; but, at a time when his works are being deployed in service of all manner of projects, there remains no better person to clarify his thought than Fisher himself — and it is a thought that certainly requires some clarification.

In late 2017, for instance, "Acid Communism" was taken up in the UK by a soft left contingent directly linked to the Labour Party, who attempted to further embolden a resurgent democratic socialism by combining it with an entwined rave-hippie nostalgia, even going so far as to call for a re-engagement with those aspects of hippiedom that Fisher was most suspicious of. Later renamed "Acid Corbynism" to ground it more firmly in its contemporary moment, this movement did remain loyal to many of Fisher's concerns, such as the need to raise a newly collective consciousness, but it also retained many of the qualities that Fisher saw as detrimental to any resurgent countercultural cause.[59] This movement also failed to take into account that central problematic within all of his writings: the crisis of the negative. This is to say that collective joy is a superficial salve for an individualised melancholy if neither is capable of producing the new. We must find a way to intervene in both, in their entwined totality, that is capable of moving us forwards. By disregarding this tensile core of Fisher's dialectically psychedelic project, any posthumous "Acid Communism" is doomed to be little more than a "folk politics" — and, if the contents of the first five lectures of this course are anything to go by, Fisher had much more in store for his readers than that.

With this in mind, it is our hope that these lectures will be a useful resource, providing a broader foundation to the *Acid Communism* project than has previously been available. In many ways, it is astounding that an interest in *Acid Communism* has been stoked by so little, and especially by something so unfinished — a testament to the lucidity of Fisher's drafts, never mind his finished texts. Whilst the texts gathered here may similarly warrant the label of "drafts", they nonetheless constitute something much more than an introduction. We are presented, instead, with the (partial) unravelling of an Ariadnean thread — and this is an unravelling we are all implored to continue in his absence.

This may be an uncomfortable suggestion to some.

It is undoubtedly Fisher's capability as a guide, in this regard — his talents as a Stalker, even, traversing capitalism's weird and eerie Zones — that has led to the growing interest in his thought since his untimely death. Even those who were not familiar with his work before 2017 find themselves expressing the same sentiment that has been expressed online over and over again: "I wish Mark Fisher was here" — to guide, to inform, to give us confidence, to give us a laugh. But, in each instance, it is clear that the questions Fisher asked of Lyotard and Sleaford Mods remain pertinent to his own project as well as those inspired by his legacy. Who will make contact with the anger and frustration he articulated? In addition, who will make contact with the joy and energy he created as well? The answer to these questions is not an individual but a collective. It was not Fisher himself, but a people yet to come.

Note on the Text

The five lectures presented on the following pages were produced using recordings made and shared by Nace Zavrl.

Readers may find a new Fisher here; a Fisher that most did not know. This is an experimental Fisher, developing arguments in real time, working to convince and raise the consciousness of his students that another world is possible. This is Fisher uncut; Fisher in his element. He waxes lyrical on a wide breadth of topics and manages to engage his students with some difficult concepts. It makes sense that this, too, would be Mark's sounding board for *Acid Communism*. Just as *Capitalist Realism* had been implicitly written for his A-Level students at the further education college where he taught in the mid-2000s, in the hope it might drag them from their disenfranchised stupor, this was Mark passing on a toolkit for a new generation, or perhaps the same generation ten years later, now fully engaged and looking to cut deeper beneath the surface of mandatory individualism, touchscreen capture, and infinite drudgery.

As lectures recorded in a modern university, the original recordings are punctured by other goings-on. Instances of interruption have been retained to account for the ways in which Mark's thought would bounce around, ricochet between references, and recover itself when a particular thread had been lost. Edits have nonetheless been made, on occasion, to dampen the impact of these instances on the reading experience.

Otherwise, these transcripts attempt to stay true to spoken cadences and turns of phrase, regardless of their idiosyncratic nature. This has been done to retain Mark's voice as much as possible and, even more importantly, the lucid, dynamic and improvisatory lecturing style so loved by his students.

In other projects of this kind, it is usually a given that such inconsistencies or interruptions are scrubbed from the record, but given the work-in-progress nature of the lecture series itself and the "open experiment" that Mark declared he was inaugurating, it seems only right to try and retain the atmosphere of those early Monday mornings. They are idiosyncratic, divergent, and meandering — but they were anything but miserable.

Student identities have been removed to preserve the right to anonymity.

All quotations and page numbers referenced over the course of the sessions are related to the editions of the texts set in the weekly readings, unless otherwise stated. A full list of these readings can be found in the course syllabus, included in the present volume under Appendix One. More detailed referencing can be found in the footnotes.

Additional footnotes either contain supplementary materials — such as more precise directions to texts mentioned in passing, argument summaries, and bullet points taken from lecture slides (during week one specifically) — or otherwise provide additional information regarding some comments that may appear to be non sequiturs outside the immediate context of the classroom.

Lecture One:
What is Postcapitalism?

7 November 2016

MARK FISHER: ...We'll just go through the structure as I see it at the moment. As I say, you can contribute to it, you can shape it — it's an open experiment, this course, starting now, really...

OK. Well, what I was going to do to start off was talk about the negative inspiration for the course. I was going to play you three things, but I'll have to talk these through because the sound isn't working for a reason I can't understand...

(*Fisher plays Apple's 1984 Super Bowl commercial, in which a woman wearing colourful sportswear, chased by security guards in riot gear, hurls a sledgehammer into a giant screen, before which sits an army of expressionless grey drones, reminiscent of an address by Big Brother in George Orwell's 1984. At the end, the advert declares: "On January 24th, Apple Computer will introduce Macintosh. And you'll see why 1984 won't be like '1984'".[1]*)

This is the first one — anyone recognise this? Anyone seen this before? (*General murmuring.*) Yeah. It features in the Steve Jobs film, doesn't it? Has anyone encountered it before that?... Yeah? Where have you seen it?

STUDENT #1: Well, I haven't seen the Steve Jobs film...

MF: Oh, you haven't seen the Steve Jobs film...

STUDENT #1: ...But I think someone posted it on Facebook, I guess? I don't have a context here; I just know that it's an Apple Super Bowl commercial.

MF: Yeah, it's definitely worth watching later with the sound... As I say, I can't fix the sound at the moment... The image itself tells the story here. I often polemically say, "This is the most influential film from the last thirty-five years". It was made by... Anyone know who directed that?

STUDENT #2: Ridley Scott.

MF: Yeah, so Ridley Scott directed it and you can tell, can't you? You can tell from the style it's very similar to films that he'd recently made. He had redefined mainstream Hollywood cinematic science fiction via *Alien* and *Blade Runner*, from '79 and '82 I think, so this was two years after that. It's really the best film he's made since then, I think. Probably the only significant film he's made since then.

What this did, really, was seed the idea of many of the tropes that are now, I think, standard in our imagining: the idea of top-down, bureaucratic control systems versus the dynamism of a kind of networked individual mindset.

And what is clever, I think — or certainly significant — all advertising you could say is a form of dreamwork — dreamwork, as Freud says, involves conflation, and a compressing, a condensing of different ideas together. All this does, if you look at the imagery, is it condenses Cold War imagery — which none of you are really old enough to actually remember except historically, I think — Cold War imagery associated with the Soviet Union in particular; negative imagery to do with dreariness, bureaucratic submission of individuals. If you look at the film, these grey drones trudge around being subjected to the ultimately top-down commands coming from the talking head, clearly referencing *1984* of Orwell. (The Orwell estate wasn't too happy about the ad but that's another story — we'll leave that aside.[2]) But it conflates that imagery that has long been associated with the Soviet bloc, with imagery to do with big computer corporations, such as IBM, which then dominated the computer world.

Apple is positioning itself as an upstart, as colour intervening into this grey, dreary, bureaucratic world. Apple is new. It's female, interestingly. It's colour intervening in this grey world of bureaucratic monoliths where IBM becomes, in the advertising dreamwork, equated with the Soviet Union. This, then, is the new world that is about to break out of this monolithic, dreary, grey, boring control system. And that's what happened! In a certain way, it was prophetic. It was more than prophetic; you could say it was hyperstitional.[3] It helped to bring about the very thing which it was describing.

From my point of view, what I think is interesting about this, then, is the way in which it suggests there is a problem of desire in terms of capital. The thing about the Cold War imagery — what it's suggesting is there is no real desire for... Or rather, there is *only* desire for capitalism. The Communist world, like IBM, and the then dominant corporate capitalist world, is boring and dreary, and that's an objection to it! The new capitalist world won't be like that. The new capitalist world will be about desire in a way that the Communist world won't be.

So that was part of the interest for me in that. I put the PowerPoint [presentation] up on the VLE[4] so you can watch it with sound later. It's just inevitable you get these bloody problems — actually immediately disproving the underlying message of that: that Apple and Microsoft would be smooth and glitch-free. We've

spent five minutes here and we know that isn't the case...
(*Laughter.*) So I can't see any reason why that sound isn't
working, but it isn't...

Right. The second thing I wanted to show was this
commercial from, I think, a similar time. Anyone seen
this one? (*Mark plays "Levi's 1984 Russia".*[5] *As it plays, he
describes some of the commercial's key features, in which a
man nervously passes through border control in Russia, as
Soviet guards rifle through his case, unearthing Western
magazines. Interrupted by the arrival of a superior, they
allow the man through who breathes a heavy sigh of relief as
he enters into the Soviet Union and, later, his flat, removing a
hidden pair of Levi's blue jeans from his suitcase.*)

He's got his case there... a copy of *The Face*, then
the style bible, the leading magazine of style culture
in London... Here he is in his dreary Soviet world. It's
all black and white. Look at his miserable flat that he's
going to. *Oh, but look!* (*Laughter.*) His life is redeemed
because he's managed to smuggle the Levi's into the
Soviet Union.

This wasn't just something made up for the
commercial. Levi's did have that super-fetishised quality
in the Soviet Union. So, again, what is this pointing
to? The fact that it's not only that the Soviet bloc was
repressive — politically repressive — it also inhibits
desire and blocks desire.

These commercials came out, then, at what, in
retrospect, we can see was the end of the Cold War. It
didn't seem like it was towards the end then, in the
middle of the Eighties. The collapse of the Soviet Union
and the Soviet system was so quick at the end of the
Eighties, no one would have foreseen it from the middle
of the Eighties. It still felt like a full-on Cold War that
would continue for decades at that point.

So those came from that period. The third thing I was

going to show you, which there's no point showing you at all without the sound...

STUDENT #3: Can I just ask — where was the Levi's ad shown?

MF: It was shown in the UK. It was a UK ad. Yeah. It was made for the UK.

(*Mark plays a clip from Louise Mensch's 2010 appearance on the UK comedy panel show,* Have I Got News for You.[6])

This is former Tory MP and so-called "chick lit" author Louise Mensch — I can't believe she's called "Mensch"; it's like a daft Martin Amis character, isn't it? — Louise Mensch who appeared on *Have I Got News for You*, the fairly lame, satirical BBC political show, at the time of Occupy London.

What she famously claimed was that the protesters of Occupy had no authenticity or validity because they went into Starbucks, and also maybe they had iPhones. Certainly, others said that. They've got iPhones and therefore they can't really be anti-capitalist.

So, there's a lineage, isn't there, I think, from those first two commercials into the Louise Mensch position. There's a narrative behind it, which is a story about desire. These protesters have the products of advanced capitalism, therefore... it's not only that they're hypocrites, it's that they don't really want what they say they want. They don't really want a wealth beyond capitalism. What they want is all of the fruits of capitalism — and ultimately that's why capitalism will win. They may claim, ethically, that they want to live in a different world but libidinally, at the level of desire, they are committed to living within the current capitalist world.

These three things are the negative inspiration for the course, where I'm going to pose the question: is there really a desire for something beyond capitalism? And partly this is informed, then, by recent debates on accelerationism, and this is probably the biggest influence on the course which I was introduced to in two phases, really. The first was in the Nineties when I was closely exposed to the work of Nick Land, who we'll look at later, a very controversial figure who developed a form of — I don't want to say right-wing, exactly — capitalistic accelerationism. His idea was that capital was the most intense force ever to exist on earth — that the whole of terrestrial history had led to the emergence of this effectively planetary artificial intelligence system which therefore can be seen as retrospectively guiding all of history towards its own emergence — a bit like Skynet in the *Terminator* films.

Land's work is this intense poeticisation of the power of capital. It's interesting that that work came out in the Nineties at that moment of the high triumph of capital, after the collapse of the Soviet system at the end of the Eighties. Land's work was really a play on — a development of — a kind of remix of earlier, ostensibly left-wing thought — particularly the work of Deleuze and Guattari and Lyotard — and they tried to imagine precisely a kind of postcapitalism that would try not to involve retreating from capitalist modernity but trying to go all the way through it.

It was in the last few years that that left-wing idea of accelerationism... The term "accelerationism" itself was invented initially as a negative term by Benjamin Noys' book *The Persistence of the Negative*; was repurposed by Alex Williams and Nick Srnicek... (*Mark emphasises the pronunciation of "Srnicek" as "sur-nek".*) That's how we pronounce it, which is from the horse's mouth. I think Nick's ancestors, when they moved to Canada, gave up trying to get Canadians to pronounce it correctly.

(*Laughter.*) But anyway, they tried to repurpose this idea of accelerationism, this move into postcapitalism from a left-wing perspective — and actually there was a seminar here, a symposium here at Goldsmiths four or five years ago, where Nick and Alex, I think, really started to develop those ideas.

So that basic question — the question behind a lot of the debates surrounding accelerationism — is postcapitalism imaginable? Is it possible to retain some of the libidinal, technological infrastructure of capital and move beyond capital? Those are the debates that have shaped my thinking over the last few years — probably one of the most important debates to shape my thinking — and therefore also shape the structure of the course.

I'll just briefly go over the thinking of the structure of the fifteen weeks. So, this week we're looking at three different accounts of postcapitalism. What is postcapitalism? I don't think we'll know by the end of today, but we'll hear a bit about the three different accounts of postcapitalism: Nick and Alex's, Gibson-Graham's, and Paul Mason's. Paul Mason's is a kind of syncretic account, really, based on lots of different theories, and I think the reading from this week is typical of the mix of reading that I want on the course: somewhat theoretical, somewhat journalistic, also some cultural and political history as well. It's not a heavily theoretical course, I don't think... At least not "*theory*" as such every week...

So, this week — a general introduction. Then, after that, I'm taking a broadly chronological approach. Part of what I want to look at is a lot of what is behind the accelerationist debates but hasn't really come out into the open, which is to do with a more aesthetic side of the question, which I think we can see certainly in the work of Lyotard and Deleuze and Guattari, etc., in the Seventies, to some extent emerging out of the pressure coming out of the counterculture of the Sixties and into the Seventies; the potential fusion of the counterculture with the left. We hear about this a lot from May '68 and all of that — I'm kind of displacing May '68, a little bit, in the narrative of this course.[7] I'm more interested in the Seventies in lots of ways — the Seventies in the US partly but also the Seventies in Italy — and thinking about what would happen if this fusion of the counterculture and left-wing politics had been more successful; had persisted. We'll look at some moments where it flourished, temporarily, but it didn't persist. And, in fact, the period that we're looking at is the period of neoliberal triumph.

So, what I want to look at next week is two approaches for that, really. Marcuse, who I'm seeing as really prefiguring the counterculture. Marcuse's book *Eros and Civilization* is incredible! I realised when I was thinking about this over the weekend — I've already mentioned Deleuze and Guattari a couple of times but they're not on the reader. They are the spectres behind a lot of what we're doing. It's almost perverse that we had to leave them out... It's because they're already there in a certain form... But I also think it's interesting to look at Marcuse as a kind of precursor of Deleuze and Guattari, with the question of taking on Freud and desire, and the question of desire... Marcuse's incredible book *Eros and Civilization* is out of print, interestingly like a lot of Marcuse's work... Marcuse, from selling hundreds of thousands of copies of *One-Dimensional Man* — still in print — regarded as a major work, and now, as I say, a lot of his work is out of print. I think Marcuse was widely read in the counterculture because his work anticipated a lot of the strands of the counterculture.

So next week I want to play that off against Ellen Willis, who's a journalist and cultural critic, who lived through the counterculture but also saw similar limitations of it. And what I particularly like about this piece by Ellen Willis is how it raises the question of what we'll look at later; of what Helen Hester calls "domestic realism", which is a bit of a parallel to what I've called "capitalist realism" — i.e. the idea that domestic structures, the ways we organise our lives at home, are fixed and immutable, and we can't imagine them being any different. In the Sixties, in the counterculture, people did try to live in a different way, did try to live in a more collective and communal way. It didn't work out. It stalled. It failed. It went wrong. Interestingly, Willis's argument is that part of the problem was impatience. People thought that we could overcome these structures very quickly. In fact, they are highly tenacious and will reassert themselves unless they are continually dismantled.

OK. So that's setting up certain coordinates, then, between the counterculture and the left, and I think that's the kind of democratic socialism or libertarian communism that Marcuse wanted — and Marcuse was a heavy critic of the actually-existing Soviet system.

Part of what I also want to think about on this course, then — or module I should call it — is the question of consciousness, which I think has receded in recent years. What I called "capitalist realism", you could say, which is the shadow of this course — it's called "Postcapitalist Desire" but it's also about capitalist realism and the rise of capitalist realism. As capitalist realism rises, as the idea that there's no alternative to capitalism becomes the ambient political assumption — in order for that to be the case, consciousness has to recede. Consciousness in the sense of — initially as theorised by Lukács in terms of "class consciousness" — but Nancy Hartsock's invaluable work on consciousness from a socialist feminist angle broadens this out not just from class consciousness but from what I would call a subordinate "group consciousness", and the importance of this.

Marcuse, in the section of reading which I've given for Week 2, talks about the spectre of a society which could be free, and I think this is almost a proto-accelerationist section of his work. He's saying, OK, once the problem of scarcity is resolved — which it effectively is under late capitalism: the problem is not that there isn't enough food to feed everybody, the problem is the distribution of the food. Scarcity isn't the problem, it's actually the maintaining of scarcity which is the problem for capitalism. The production of an artificial scarcity in order to conceal abundance, you could say, and a scarcity of time as much as a scarcity of actual goods, services, etc. Marcuse says, once this scarcity is overcome, capitalism has to work extremely hard at avoiding the possibility that people could determine their own lives and behave in a more autonomous way. This is, in a way, the driver of the emergence of capitalist realism, I would say — and neoliberalism is a part of that — is constantly having to thwart the potential emergence of postcapitalism, of people living in ways that are beyond the imperatives of capitalism. We'll see that Gibson-Graham argues that we're already doing that, most of the time in fact.

OK. So that, in a way, becomes a problem of inhibiting the emergence of consciousness. We'll see that in Week 3 with the reading of Lukács and Hartsock, which will then condition a lot of what we'll do in the weeks after that.

Week 4 is labour history — an incredible moment in the early Seventies when, in the US, a lot of these currents came together with a new set of demands in the workplace; when civil rights, feminism and class struggle came together. When we use the word "intersectionality" now, it just means horrible squabbles on Twitter, people calling each other out, all of that kind of thing.

It's simply about a problem where things don't actually intersect properly; where, instead of a development of a consolidated group consciousness, there are identitarian squabbles amongst these groups. What if the opposite were the case? What if it had been possible to develop a form of political struggle which would genuinely intersect all of these forms of subordination in order to overcome them? There were hints of this in the US in the early Seventies.

It's a great book, this — a great book of cultural theory — it's not really theory, it's cultural-political history of recent years — Jefferson Cowie's book, *Stayin' Alive: The 1970s and the Last Days of the Working Class*. A book of two halves, very much: the first half devoted to the positive explosion of libertarian communism, existential leftism, etc., and the second half about the defeat of the feeling of the New Left as well as the Old Left. The Old Left was swindled, and the New Left was stymied.

Following on from that, then, Lyotard's text "The Desire Named Marx" from his infamous — what you can call later his "evil" book — *Libidinal Economy*. It makes the case, a particularly strong case, that there's no possible retreat from capitalism — there's no space of primitive outside to which we can return, we have to go all the way through capitalism. He makes this claim super specifically.

Then we focus on Italy, with Federici and Nicolas Thoburn's account of the refusal of work. You'll see how some of this played out on the ground, particularly in Italy in the Seventies.

The next few weeks after that we'll devote to the counter-revolution itself, where we see postcapitalist desire in negative, I think, via the shadow it casts. If we can talk about this last forty or fifty years now as being shaped by the spectre of a world which could be free, then we can see that spectre in the ways in which capital has set itself up to thwart the emergence of consciousness, autonomy, and the refusal of work. The horrific testing ground for that is, first of all, Chile — a democratic socialist project, close to the US, very different from anything to do with the Soviet bloc, technologised, had the so-called socialist internet, CyberSyn, in place, destroyed... It can't be said, "ah, it didn't work, what happened in Chile". It didn't work because there was a CIA-backed coup to destroy it — the military destruction of the Allende government in Chile — which I think then provides a kind of prototype for what would happen afterwards. In places like the UK, it wasn't quite so immediately violent. There was violence — the Miners' Strike, etc. — but it was a kind of capitalist-realist lab which allowed capital to experiment with these new forms of subjection.

Week 8: we look at what I've called "the invention of the middle", based on Carl Freedman's book *The Age of Nixon* and Penny Lewis's book *Hard Hats, Hippies and Hawks*. In a way, this is about the suppression of consciousness again — specifically of class consciousness.

The role that I think Nixon played in this, if you read Carl's book, is in generalising a form of what Marx had characterised as a "petit bourgeois psychology", which is the idea of being in a class position which sets you up outside class altogether — "there is a class system but you don't really belong to it". This is the appeal that Nixon made to people — the so-called "Middle America" — which encouraged people to see themselves as part of and from this petit bourgeois perspective, which could then be generalised as a form of suppressing class consciousness. So, workers started to see themselves in terms of the petit bourgeoisie and Nixon could plausibly make this pitch because of his own background. Unlike

Kennedy, for instance, he didn't come from a great privileged background — he worked his way up — and this is key to the petit bourgeois psychology: the idea that you can produce your own position in society through hard work.

We'll look at the way in which Nixon, despite his ultimate humiliation and failure — nevertheless the Nixon paradigm became something that has continued to this day. Mrs Thatcher was very similar to Nixon in lots of ways — similar background, similar values, similar advocacy of this general petit bourgeois psychology — and we'll see how this played out in terms of this image of hard hats versus hippies. I think it was 1970, some construction workers famously attacked anti-Vietnam War protestors, producing this image of a reactionary working class versus effete students, which continues to this day, really. And the workers are therefore on the side of the "Middle", of the silent majority of Middle America, etc. and this production of a "middle", then, produces a paradoxical space. How can everyone belong to the middle? It's impossible. When John Prescott, the New Labour politician said, "we're all middle class now"... well, if everyone's middle class now then what are they in the middle of? But it seems to make sense — this pitch — as a form of direct suppression of class consciousness.

Then we'll go on to "Post-Fordism and New Times" — Stuart Hall theorising New Times from one perspective, Virno and the Italian post-autonomists theorising from another. Post-Fordism, then, is the big shift in the infrastructure of capitalism — a shift towards what we now call precarity, flexibility, flexibilisation, casualisation, etc. and info-technology becoming central. We'll look at that there, in Week 9.

Week 10: technofeminism; cyberfeminism — this, then, is part of the genealogy of accelerationism —

cyberfeminism, the technofeminism of Firestone, who really thought that a lot of the problems of gender were material and technologically resolvable. So, for instance, once it's possible to have children from artificial wombs, that would obviously radically shift gender relations, etc. Compare her to Sadie Plant from the Nineties, which you can regard in some ways perhaps as a neoliberal form of cyberfeminism. Sadie Plant worked closely with Nick Land in the Nineties, actually. I've skipped out the most famous cyberfeminism, which is Donna Haraway, because I think you probably know about that anyway and we'll look at either side of that. You can fill that bit in for yourself. A bit like Deleuze and Guattari — they can be added in as an extra bit.

But onto Week 11: accelerationism. I hadn't chosen Nick and Alex because we'll look at them now and they informed the whole of the course, really. But we will look at Jameson's piece "Utopia as Replication" where he makes the famous — well, not that famous — the (in some quarters) famous claim, looking at Walmart as a form of utopia... Dialectical thinking... Really classic accelerationist move, which is to say, what if the infrastructure of Walmart was repurposed for entirely different purposes... That's a bad sentence... Repurposed for entirely different ends. And Nick Land's "Machinic Desire", which is the classic statement of his form of accelerationism. So, it's a kind of left- and right-accelerationism in closing there.

So, a lot of the accelerationist debate actually came out of the impasses or failures of the anti-capitalist political movements since 2008. Part of that is to do with horizontalism —which was the critique of the idea of hierarchical structures. There's something problematic about the hierarchical structures of political organisation. When they are instantiated, they are already oppressive.

So if we want to prefigure a postcapitalist world, we must be horizontalist. We must work to always eliminate hierarchies wherever they appear. A lot of the left-accelerationist stuff came out of a dissatisfaction of this.

Part of this thinking is, then, a kind of fusion of anarchist currents with network theory. One example of this is this kind of peer-to-peer politics, which is Week 13, and Michel Bauwens is probably the most famous example of that. We'll also look at the most famous thinkers of the network in Week 12: Hardt and Negri, the unofficial theoretical — what's a non-hierarchical way of putting this? — the "inspiration" behind Occupy, etc.

Hardt and Negri, of course, had been involved, in Italy in the 1970s, with Autonomia and those struggles.[8] So, there is a direct lineage back to the sort of stuff we looked at earlier. Then we'll look at Jodi Dean's critique of this. We'll spend two weeks looking at the network. First of all, a long section from *Commonwealth* [by Hardt and Negri] — which I think is their best book, actually — and then we'll look at peer-to-peer and we'll look at Jodi Dean's critique of all this.

Week 14: back in the bleak — "Touchscreen Capture", as I've called it — then looking at Baudrillard, who I think gives an astonishingly prescient account of the "tactile power" as he calls it.[9] "They come to touch", he says. Read a lot of his passages from the Seventies and it reads astonishingly like he's time-travelled into now and he's talking about Twitter and the touchscreen interface.

Next to that, Franco Berardi's famous critique of current conditions of info-labour and precarity. Berardi: one of the few contemporary thinkers who takes Baudrillard seriously.

Then, to end it on a more positive note: "Prometheus Reborn" — although that's probably a too organic way of putting it. I think some of these currents come together in an exciting way in the *Xenofeminist Manifesto* from 2015 — so only last year — and Helen Hester's piece "Promethean Labours and Domestic Realism". I think this offers all sorts of exciting possibilities for a postcapitalist politics at the current moment, so we'll try to end it on a positive note.

So that's the thinking behind the whole structure... Any questions on that? Just interrupt me at any time. I hope I don't speak as much in the future weeks, but we need to warm up, I guess. Does that make sense? Is that sort of what you were expecting or is anyone crushingly disappointed with that? (*Laughter.*)

What's absent from it I think, and what I want to be more present — you can perhaps bring this in — is the question of aesthetics, artwork, and culture, and its role in all of this, which I think is key, and had been underestimated by elements of the so-called Old Left.

Let's go on to today, then, because otherwise we'll never get through everything. I've basically just summarised some of the key claims... OK, before we get to that... I've got way too much stuff but never mind. It's better to have too much than too little.

OK. So, what are the advantages of the concept of postcapitalism?[10] — and just initially I think it's worth thinking about this — why use the term "postcapitalism" rather than "communism", "socialism", etc.? Well, first of all, it's not tainted by association with past failed and oppressive projects. The term "postcapitalism" has a kind of neutrality that is not there with "communism", "socialism". Although this is partly generational, I think: the word "communism" has lots of negative associations for people of my age and older.

It implies victory — that's the other thing, isn't it? If you're talking about postcapitalism, it implies that there's something beyond capitalism. It also implies direction, doesn't it? If it's postcapitalism, it's a victory and a victory that will come *through* capitalism. It's not just *opposed to* capitalism — it is what *will* happen when capitalism has ended. It starts from where we are. It's not some entirely separate space — I think that's implied, right? The concept of postcapitalism is something developed *out* of capitalism. It develops *from* capitalism and moves *beyond* capitalism. Therefore, we're not required to imagine a *sheer alterity*, a *pure* outside. That's one of the emphases of postcapitalism. We can begin with, work with, the pleasures of capitalism, as well as its oppressions. So, we're not necessarily trapped in this Louise Mensch world where, if we have iPhones, we can't want postcapitalism. Although I don't think we'd want iPhones in postcapitalism...

Anyway — yes?

STUDENT #4: But doesn't it sound a bit more like a theory, in comparison to a political system?

MF: It sounds more like a theory? That's a potential problem with it, yeah. Actually, I've got a few problems with it...[11] (*Gesturing towards points made on slide.*) I've sort of said that with the second [point] there. I think you're making a slightly different point...

STUDENT #4: Because socialism and communism have an active...

MF: Yeah, it's a positive actual project, whereas postcapitalism might be too theoretical. Also, it's tied to capitalism. That's also a problem — potentially. Gibson-Graham talk about "capitalocentrism". If we're talking about postcapitalism, then, if we're framing the outcome of our political, cultural, social ambitions in terms of postcapitalism, they're still defined in relation to capitalism. So, it doesn't relate to a positive project.

(*Reading slide.*) "It remains in the temporality of the 'post-'". So, it sounds like "postmodern" — it's defined by something that preceded it rather than what it actually is itself. It's not necessarily progressive... In this new book from Verso, *Four Futures: Life After Capitalism*, I think some of it's online — [the book makes the case that] just because something is postcapitalist doesn't mean it is desirable.[12] "Extinction" is one of the phrases or models for postcapitalism [put forward in the book]. Another is a kind of high-rent super-capitalist form of accumulation that is in some sense not calculable anymore...

We might add to these. You might have some of your own.

Yeah? Please...

STUDENT #5: Yeah, I have two more...

MF: Two more? Two more problems?! OK.

STUDENT #5: Yeah... It's not only that it does not name a positive project, but it does not also name a negative project. For example, some negative aspects of capitalism that we would want to refuse. I have, in my mind, the strategies of refusal of the Autonomists, for example. Also, it is really easy to be lost inside this prefix of post-. Some postmodern narrative... Not to define anything at all. Just to talk about some postcapitalism that may fall from the sky.

MF: Yeah, I think these are all potential issues with the course.

We can think about these as we develop. You probably have more, which we can add as we carry on. Some of you might want to write on this anyway: generally, is the concept of postcapitalism "good"? Is it worth persisting with?

I've alternated. I was firmly against using anything in terms to do with "communism" a few years ago, because of the tainting problem, I think, more than anything else. But I've been persuaded that it's the very antagonism, the very alterity of the term "communism" that gives it its potential power.

STUDENT #4: Why should it be like communism anyway? To use an old...

MF: Yeah. I think when it's paired with new terms — that's what makes it interesting. The emergence of things like "Luxury Communism" as a formula, because it's immediately... Maybe we'll talk about Luxury Communism later on in the course...[13] I think what's powerful about that is it deflects or defuses — or not defuses but its opposite: explodes — the current conceptions of things or the standard stereotypes — exactly what we looked at with that dreary, grey imagery associated with the communist Soviet system. How could that be luxury? It's a kind of cognitive bomb — something like Luxury Communism.

I've also been trying to work on a concept of "Acid Communism". That's what Deleuze and Guattari argue, and that's some of what we'll look at with the Jefferson Cowie stuff... The early Seventies... Psychedelic consciousness plus class consciousness... That's what capital feared in the late Sixties, early Seventies: what if the working class become hippies? Because, surely, key to the counterculture, for all its failings — and it had many — was an anti-work ethic, mainstreaming an anti-work ethic. The Beatles did it. "Stay in bed... Float upstream..."

was anti-work. And also, this question of anti-work and anti-being-busy — a different existential mode — and also this question of communal living.

So, I guess my current position would be, yeah, use "communism" with a modifier to break out of the existing associations, which a lot of young people don't have anyway, as I said, but you don't seem happy with that...

STUDENT #4: Yeah, no. I think it's super difficult. There was a socialist system... If you're in Germany or in Austria or whatever, you still kind of know what it was about, and it's still very difficult to work with those terms.

MF: I think it's partly a strategic question, isn't it? About when these terms can be used in what context...

STUDENT #4: Yeah, yeah, of course...

MF: ...and what force they can exert. It may be that they don't have universal applicability...

OK, so these are the big questions but let's turn to specifics... Oh no... (*Laughter as there are more technical difficulties.*)

OK. So, I got this from online. (*Mark brings up two diagrams, detailing a wide range of intersecting and contemporary ideas regarding postcapitalism, including their influences and related projects.*) You can see the range of different forms of postcapitalism... And almost none of those are ones that I've been talking about... (*Laughter.*) It's worth looking at later in more detail...[14]

OK, so let's look at some of the reading from today...

Gibson-Graham — I think one of the important things they highlight is the problems on the left of facing an attempt to theorise, imagine — imagine is probably a better word than theorise — a way out of capitalism. So, first there is this suspicious, paranoid, strong theory [of postcapitalism], which they get from Sedgewick:

> While it affords the pleasures of recognition, of capture, of intellectually subduing that one last thing, it offers no relief or exit to a place beyond. If we want to cultivate new habits of thinking for a postcapitalist politics, it seems there is work to be done to loosen the structure of feeling that cannot live with uncertainty or move beyond hopelessness.[15]

What they're saying, then, Gibson-Graham, is that this [failure of the imagination] is a pathology of the left itself. This is associated with left melancholia. If people have not read Wendy Brown's essay on left melancholia, it's really worth looking at — it's what they're referring to extensively here. So, as they put it:

> ...in which attachment to a past political analysis or identity is stronger than the interest in present possibilities for mobilization, alliance, or transformation. Certainly, the left has experienced monumental losses, and perhaps ultimately a loss of confidence — in the viability of state socialism, the resiliency of social democracy, the credibility of Marxism, the buoyancy and efficacy of solidarity movements. Rather than grieving and letting go, the melancholic subject identifies with lost ideals, experiencing their absence as feelings of desolation and dejection... 'We come to love our left passions and reasons, our left analyses and convictions, more than we love the existing world that we presumably seek to alter'. [16]

I think anyone who's read any account of left-wing politics

will recognise these pathologies, right? In our fixation on the past — which I think is related to this problem of the inability to deal with the contingencies and uncertainties of the present — there's a clear relationship to paranoid total theory, which in effect says nothing can happen — it's what I call a harsh Leninist superego, which I think is related to this — a harsh Leninist superego was out in force when Syriza emerged in Greece — harsh Leninist superego: "This isn't gonna work!" — well, it didn't work, but it's better that it was tried than it wasn't tried, you could say. The harsh Leninist superego is out in force with Jeremy Corbyn of the Labour Party — "oh, this isn't going to work, this kind of thing doesn't work..." Well, what would work? Only a complete transformation of everything, which is not really imaginable. So, what typically happens is there is a model of political transformation — a Bolshevik sort — which is positive. That's the only way to really change things, and anything that falls short of that will be regarded as having failed. Of course, the fact that the Bolshevik revolution ultimately failed — and failed straight away, some would argue — is not going to reckon into this at all...

I can strongly sympathise with what they're seeing there — this left melancholia...

Now moralism, I think, then... Another important essay by Wendy Brown that they refer to is "Wounded Attachments".[17] "Wounded Attachments" is highly prophetic of aspects of today's left-wing world, really. What Brown does in "Wounded Attachments" is draw upon Nietzsche to show that the ways in which certain kinds of left-wing desire have been mobilised, such that identities are defined in relation to a kind of wounding. Moralism, they say:

> provides an emotional shoring up of the reactive stance

of the weak, 'who define themselves in opposition to the strong'. With the dissolution in recent times of positive projects of socialist construction, left moralism has been energized by increasing investments in injury, failure, and victimhood. When power is identified with what is ruthless and dominating, it becomes something the left must distance itself from, lest it be co-opted or compromised.[18]

So, the idea there is, then, that power itself is pathological. To hold power is to inherently be oppressive, therefore it's better to be wounded; it's better to be the wounded, the abject, because you're not actually holding power, which is oppressive. This becomes the name for a kind of impossible desire in lots of ways. Who are these appeals aimed at? What is a political project which doesn't aim at capturing power or building power in some way? I think we can recognise the ways in which this form of desire has shaped a lot of left-wing politics recently. Brown's essay is highly profound; both of those: "Wounded Attachments" and the one on left melancholia, which builds on [Walter] Benjamin's discussion of left melancholia.[19]

So, in a way, in the place of a positive political project, we have a moralistic project of condemnation. We condemn those in power:

Fearing implication with those in power, we become attached to guarding and demonstrating our purity rather than mucking around in everyday politics. Those who engage in such work may find themselves accused of betraying their values, sleeping with the enemy, bargaining with the devil — all manner of transgressions and betrayals.[20]

It's interesting how that accusation comes from two

angles, you could say — one is from this position of the wounded, who say you should never truck with existing power, and also comes from the position of those who would have *ultimate* power, like Leninists. They would make the same criticism as well. Don't be tempted by any attempt to engage with the currently existing political structures or structures of power because you'll be compromised by that.

And then they... I mean, I like their analysis but the films [they reference] are awful, aren't they? (*Laughter.*) I doubt anyone who's not British will have seen *Brassed Off*, but you've probably seen *The Full Monty* — have you? Yeah? Yeah! It's incredible how they literally say they're ecstatic about the film. Those films: I can't say I like 'em... (*Laughter.*) I've sort of gone against my aesthetic preferences, I think, in including them. (*Laughs.*) But it's the analysis I think, then... I think they write something similar with *Brassed Off*... I don't think you've seen that film, but you feel like you know what it's about... You know, brass band and colliery... It's all there, this kind of left melancholia... Detached political nostalgia for these older forms of masculine labour... You know, this fixation on... I think that part of the problem is this fixation on resistance action, which is part of this kind of reactive model — capital does stuff, we resist it. I think they rightly identify the impasses of this "modernist class politics",[21] as they call it, in something like *Brassed Off*, which exemplifies a lot of their critique.

According to them, then: dislocation...[22] Moving beyond capitalocentrism:

> We can begin to 'unfix' economic identity by deconstructing the dominant capitalocentric discourse of economy in which capitalist economic activity is taken as the model for all economic activity. We can dislocate the unity

and hegemony of neoliberal global capitalist economic discourse through a proliferative queering of the economic landscape and construction of a new language of economic diversity.[23]

I think the key thing for them is there's no such thing as "The Economy". The economy — the definite article — is fake. It is a kind of fiction; a kind of operative fiction which secures capitalist hegemony. At the level of empirical reality, there are multiple economic activities, but at the level of hegemonic narrative, it's all about capitalism. So capitalocentrism is what capital does, but I think they worry about reproducing it in terms of left-wing theory and practices.

So they've got this model there.[24] If we look at what goes on in the world, they say — "wage labour produce for a market in a capitalist firm"[25] is a tiny thing, when we look at all the other forms of work that go on — in schools, on the street, in neighbourhoods, families, unpaid, time between friends... You get the basic point...

If you take this model, then, there is not *one* economy, there's lots of different forms of engagement with production. So, there must be economies that are already non-capitalist. So they argue that it's partly to escape what I call the harsh Leninist superego or these Leninist models.[26] They think that what we need is alternative organisational forms inspired by feminist experimentation: "Organizational horizontalism... direct and equitable participation, non-monopoly of the spoken word or of information, the rotation of occasional tasks and responsibilities, the non-specialization of functions, the non-delegation of power".[27]

The thing is, then, you could make massive change — that's what this second large quote is saying — without the need for a vanguard party, like the Leninists thought.

By "Leninism" simply meaning the idea of: the revolution will be led by a small elite in a political party — the party organises the subordinated class and leads them. They're arguing for this more horizontalist model, then, coming out of feminism: "embodied practices, self-cultivation, emplaced actions", etc.[28] So, a new set of affects[29]: "[The affects associated with this] becoming community are not those traditionally linked to left politics..."[30] So not outrage and anger; not cynicism and righteousness; wonder, delight, etc. "In this utopian atmosphere, distrust, misrecognition, and judgment are temporarily suspended and a solidarity develops that is based not on sameness, but on a growing recognition that the other is what makes self possible".[31]

I'm really desperate to get out of *The Full Monty* now. It's astonishing.

In *The Full Monty*, you know what happens, right? It's in Sheffield, isn't it, I think? Yeah? Northern town in England, anyway... Big problem with unemployment... Men are miserable — what do they do? — they decide to take up stripping, basically... So, Gibson-Graham, for them, this releases this new affect... A release from this old form of masculinity — which is good! — but I think it's Žižek's critique, which they mention: is this not just a form of entrepreneurialism? Is this not just a form of flagellation? "The factories have closed, let's just make our own business..." They're getting something different from that, which they're referring to... I think the important thing to take from this is that these other forms of affect are important.

Part of the story, I would say — a big part of the story that I want to be pushing over this module is: what is the alternative to *ressentiment*? We'll talk about this when we look at Carl Freedman's work on Nixon. The neoliberal programme — despite its emphasis on freedom — is really, I think, a lot about *ressentiment*.[32] What are the alternatives to that? Solidarity is one word for that, but I think it's tainted by association with Leninism, for me. What about a word like "fellowship"? How does that develop? What are the spaces and conditions for that? I think this is one thing I'd like you to get out of the seminar.

So, they talk about the community economy versus the mainstream or capitalist economy.[33] (I'm going to speed up a bit through the rest of the book.) These are the kind of principles they're talking about: surviving together well and equitably; distributing surplus to enrich social and environmental health; encountering others in ways that support their well-being as well as ours; consuming sustainably; caring for — maintaining, replenishing, and growing — our natural and cultural commons; investing our wealth in future generations so that they can live as well...

> An Economy centered on these ethical considerations is what we call a community economy — a space of decision making where we recognize and negotiate our interdependence with other humans, other species, and our environment. In the process of recognizing and negotiating, we become a community.[34]

This is their model of postcapitalism. Notice how some of this sounds like uncontroversial, mainstream rhetoric... Bank adverts could incorporate this model... Sustainability... It doesn't mean they're really going to do it but that indicates some of the pressure that some of these discourses are having on the mainstream...

OK. Is this just "folk politics", though? I guess this is the question...

So, there's their diagram of "The Economy" versus the

community economy.[35] So economy is aspatial and global; community is place-attached... Economy is specialised; community is diversified... Economy is centred; community economy is decentred... Privately owned; community owned... etc. You get the picture.

But is this just folk politics? This concept of folk politics, then, [was] developed by Alex Williams and Nick Srnicek, partly because of the failures of post-2008/2009 anti-capitalism. There was a certain level of success that the groups managed to achieve but that was limited and, according to Nick and Alex, one of the reasons for that was the effect of folk politics. They argue that:

> the most important division in today's left is between those that hold to a folk politics of localism, direct action, and relentless horizontalism, and those that outline what must be called an accelerationist politics at ease with a modernity of abstraction, complexity, globality, and technology. The former remains content with establishing small and temporary spaces of non-capitalist social relations, eschewing the real problems entailed in facing foes which are intrinsically non-local, abstract, and rooted deep in our everyday infrastructure. The failure of such politics has been built-in from the very beginning. By contrast, an accelerationist politics seeks to preserve the gains of late capitalism while going further than its value system, governance structures, and mass pathologies will allow.[36]

Are Gibson-Graham folk politics in that sense?

STUDENT #6: Sorry, could you repeat that?

MF: Oh, it was partly rhetorical. Is what Gibson-Graham are proposing folk politics in that sense?

Take the term folk politics: it comes from a critique of folk psychology that was developed by neurophilosophers. Neurophilosophers argue that folk psychology is no good — the concepts that we have in everyday life — including things even like emotions — the way we describe what goes on in our brains is no use for what *actually* goes on in our brains, and really inhibits the study of what the brain actually does. In the same way, then, Nick and Alex are taking this analogy [and applying it to a] political process, arguing that the spontaneous concepts that we have in everyday life to understand political systems — just simply the political economic system — have no purchase on the reality of something like capital — finance capital, etc. There's a kind of mismatch between the two. And it would seem, on the face of it, that Gibson-Graham could fall into folk politics. I don't think they fully do, actually. There is a model of hegemonic takeover. They don't think you can just operate locally. There has to be some kind of hegemonic struggle. I think we can see a tension already, then, between the approach that Nick and Alex advocate in the *Manifesto for an Accelerationist Politics* and the Gibson-Graham approach. But as they develop their argument in this book, which some of you have got — *Inventing the Future* — their claims become somewhat softer than they were in the Accelerationist manifesto.

How do we get there? We need demands. There has been this talk of a politics without demands; a demandless politics.[37] They're saying, well, demands are crucial! "A politics without demands is simply a collection of aimless bodies"[38] — a provocative claim — and these demands should take the form of *"non-reformist reforms"*.[39] These reforms have utopian and antagonistic components, and are based "in actual tendencies at work in the world today" — pragmatic interventions.[40]

So, let's quickly go through what their demands actually are.

Full automation: "Without full automation, postcapitalist futures must necessarily choose abundance at the expense of freedom (echoing the work-centricity of Soviet Russia) or the freedom at the expense of abundance represented by the primitivist utopia".[41] And how much freedom can you really have without abundance, anyway?

So, the arguments for full automation are: it can lead to a society that liberates humanity from drudgery while also increasing the amount of wealth; it is already happening (between 47 and 80% of today's jobs are capable of being automated); it can lead to a re-valuation and even elimination of certain types of care work, allowing a radical transformation of the domestic sphere...[42]

The demand for a reduced working week[43] — now, this is interesting, isn't it: how this [demand] stopped [being made]. There was pressure to get the working week down. The introduction of the weekend. Now it's kind of stuck at forty hours and going upwards, particularly in the interest of post-Fordist labour. So, it's a positive response to rising automation.

In a capitalist dystopia, which we're in at the moment, the more automation there is, the more miserable things are, right? Because it means less work; more unemployment. It means that the power of workers in jobs is weakened.

Reduced working week — advantages: less commuting, less consumption associated with going into work, it will increase the power of workers, because if the dystopian model of automation decreases the power of workers, this would increase it.

Universal basic income — it must be sufficient and universal, so it must be enough to live on. [It must be] a supplement to existing welfare arrangements, not a replacement for it — because that would be the right-wing version of universal basic income.[44]

Four key arguments for it — political transformation: the proletariat can subsist with a job which would increase net class power. Precarity is transformed into flexibility on workers' terms and, as they point out, a lot of post-Fordism was the capitalist genie responding to the wishes of workers in a malevolent way. OK, so you don't want to be bored in the factory forever; you don't want to be bored in the factory for forty years — fine, have temporary and casual labour. So, it changes how work is valued — boring, repetitive work would have to be higher paid if you've got universal basic income. If you've got universal basic income, you're not going to do boring work.

STUDENT #7: But who decides what's the boring work? I mean, maybe someone is enjoying the factory at some point...? (*Laughter.*)

MF: Maybe! The point is that workers themselves could decide what they wanted to do or not, much more. In a sense, the market can decide what is boring work.

STUDENT #8: And I guess we can see, already here in the UK, it's not really, like, optimistic...

STUDENT #7: Yeah, no, I do understand that.

MF: Yeah, it wouldn't be decided [by workers]. Market mechanisms would decide it, because you'd have to induce people to do things which some people might find [boring]... It'd be great for them, though, wouldn't it? It'd be even better for them. If some people found boring work — what most people find boring work — to be interesting, in this world they'd be much better off than they are now, right?

STUDENT #9: Can I just ask about inflation in relation to UBI?

MF: Oh God...

STUDENT #9: I'm from Finland, so they're just starting UBI, but that's to dismantle the...

MF: ...welfare state...

STUDENT #9: ...yeah, but what I was taught in high school was that once wages go up, then inflation goes up too, so we were taught it's really hard to get the great salaries because once the UBI...

MF: ... God, I don't know anything about economics, really... (*Laughs.*) I tried to skip over this! (*Laughs.*)

STUDENT #10: Maybe we are thinking in a capitalist framework... Or a Keynesian frame... And these kinds of measures need another economic frame, so maybe inflation is not an issue here? Because it would be part of another economy?

MF: Yeah, it wouldn't automatically lead to inflation, would it...? That's why it has to be sufficient. The UBI has to be sufficient for people to live on.

STUDENT #9: But say in Finland where everyone is getting €1000 a month, wouldn't it still mean — maybe I want to get more money because I want to move over to

London or whatever, and I'd still want to have my UK job, so I'd still get more and more money. You still need the higher paid jobs, or you still need someone to design an Uber app, and it's probably going to be me, I don't know, and then I'm going to be paid a lot because I'm the only one in the world doing the Uber app. So, then it's like I'm not going to get paid £2000, I'm going to get paid a lot more because everyone is getting...

MF: Yeah. But why is that a problem?

STUDENT #9: Just salaries rising, because if everyone's salaries are rising then it means the people on UBI are not going to be able to afford the things that I can afford.

MF: I think they're separate issues though, aren't they? One doesn't all of a sudden lift inequality, which is a separate issue to the inflation one, isn't it, really...?

STUDENT #9: Then I guess we're not getting rid of the welfare state... You're still entitled to UBI...

MF: Yeah, and the UBI has to be adjusted, I suppose, for it to remain sufficient...

Yeah, sorry, I was drifting off a bit, trying to think...

But I think it's also what [student #10] is saying: I think partly why they're proposing it is that it starts to shift us out of this certainly neoliberal capitalist model into some other space, which is really difficult to imagine. What would it be like if there actually was a sufficient UBI? Because it does start to flip our minds, doesn't it? The things that are available now... OK, so hang on, if we have UBI then people won't do this shit work, they won't do drudgery... Ah, well, hang on, then haven't we got automation? Doesn't automation then come in to take on the role of this drudgery? It just flips everything. So, what is the problem now — automation becomes a positivity — I know this doesn't directly answer what you were saying — but this is why it's a revolutionary reform, in that it starts to shift the basic coordinates and models of life, work, and society, etc.

STUDENT #11: Would you also get, though, some industries being really neglected and then others massively developing? For example, to be fair, the creative sector even now is less wealthy — it's interesting — but then, in this imaginary, would that be neglected altogether? Would there be any incentives?

STUDENT #9: I'm a designer and I don't do design because I get paid for it. I do it because I love to do it... And I wonder if there was UBI I would do projects that are actually valuable rather than ones I just get paid for.

STUDENT #12: Yeah, but I wonder about whether there's something there that isn't built into this value system, given this idea that we should just enjoy it. Is that a positive thing to reinforce?

MF: There's only one aspect, potentially — it's not the only thing that would necessarily be happening — because partly it's about shifting the emphasis away from remuneration altogether, isn't it? I think with Gibson-Graham the key thing is a diverse economy with Nick and Alex's post-work, right? So, you're shifting away from work and remuneration as a model anyway. So the fact that people could engage in this creative work without necessarily being remunerated at a high level — well, as we start to move into that postcapitalist world, does remuneration matter so much anyway?

STUDENT #12: So, it's more that, at the moment, it's that idea of workers being exploited in the current system…

MF: Yeah, potentially. Part of the thing is the modesty of the model, isn't it? It's moving with existing tendencies somewhere that quite quickly takes us to a place that seems far beyond where we actually are at the moment. Even though it's feasible — logistically feasible — and not that big a step. That's the cleverness of it…

So, a feminist proposal — also they're saying it allows experimentation with the family structure…

It reverses the link between suffering and remuneration.[45] I think this is key — the almost religious dimensions of what they're talking about — the Protestant work ethic, which was a kind of religious evaluation of suffering — suffering is intrinsically valuable in itself.

A counter-hegemonic approach which can draw upon already-existing hatred of jobs — and this is a photograph from a programme that was on a few years ago, which some of you might remember, called *Benefits Street* — highly controversial — typical of Channel 5, in the UK, [which] specialises in these programmes basically about people on benefits, and stoking up *ressentiment* against them, really.[46] The idea that somehow their lives are better. They can be on benefits, but it's better to be them than you — you: you belong to the hard-working middle, chipping ice off your windscreen, going to work in the winter — but what that really reveals is that people think their jobs are shit! (*Laughter.*) People hate their own jobs, and that is why they think it's better to be on benefits than in work.

OK, let's quickly go over some of the Paul Mason stuff.[47] Sorry, we're nearly running out of time. I'm trying to pack it in today.

So, Paul Mason's stuff is based on this theory of Kondratiev waves. This was the idea that capitalism renewed itself through these long waves of development — and I think he fuses this with a bit of Autonomia — theories that capitalism is partly driven by the antagonism of the working class; that when the working class resists capital, when it struggles against it, it forces capitalism to innovate. So, part of the problem at the moment would be that the very success of capitalism in subduing the working class means that it gets locked in stasis. This could account for why there's this downfall — flatlining growth rates and things like that... Economic stuff... (*Laughs.*)

I won't claim to be an expert on economics — at all. It's the cultural dimensions of this that I have a reasonable grasp on.

So, Paul Mason's stuff, really, is about information, isn't it? This is what he keeps emphasising. Peter Drucker's *Post-Capitalist Society*[48] — Peter Drucker was a management consultant. I haven't read this book — it'd be interesting to read it... The key thing is the centrality of knowledge in this post-capitalist economy. "Universal educated person" — this would be a "networked individual", according to Mason.

So, according to Mason, then, the key thing is the emergence of information and of knowledge-based goods — "info-goods"[49] — which, as he says, operate by a principle of non-rivalry. If I have this pen, you don't have it, it's physical. If I have a PDF of Mason's book, it doesn't stop you having one either. Information works like that. In lots of ways, the fact we've all got it makes it better for all of us. So, I don't lose anything by the fact that you've got it. According to him, this then introduces this new principle which is contradictory to capitalism. A basic law of economics — or of capitalist economics —

is that everything is scarce — but it isn't. You can keep replicating digital files practically *ad infinitum*. They're not scarce.

Open Source versus Microsoft: "Could Wikipedia have been created by capitalist dynamics alone?"[50] So could, by market incentivisation... Some people must be motivated by other things than profit, otherwise Wikipedia wouldn't exist. So, for him, then, a commons-based peer-to-peer production — this open source form of production — is going to threaten the capitalist, corporate model of profit-based economy.

Sorry, I'm rushing through so we can have a bit more time for discussion.

So, he refers then to "general intellect"[51] — again, the influence of Autonomia, Negri, and the like: the first to leap on the emergence of this text from Marx... ["The Fragment on Machines" from Marx's posthumously published text, the *Grundrisse*.]

General intellect: a knowledge-based society in which workers stood and supervised machines... Supervised rather than operated machines... Knowledge is socialised in this world of general intellect... So, yes, it becomes about knowledge and sociality...

Technologically, we are headed for zero-price goods, unmeasurable work, an exponential take-off in productivity and the extensive automation of physical processes. Socially, we are trapped in the world of monopolies, inefficiency, the ruin of a finance-dominated free market and a proliferation of 'bullshit jobs'.[52]

...which is David Graeber's phrase — read that essay if you've not read it, it's really good...[53]

Today, the main contradiction in modern capitalism is

between the possibility of free, abundant socially produced goods, and a system of monopolies, banks, and governments struggling to maintain control over power and information. Everything is pervaded by a fight between network and hierarchy.[54]

The fact is that capitalism — with its tendency to income inequality, information monopolies, and financial power — is running out of steam. It's time to start thinking about something new.[55]

OK. So, for him, it is this info-knowledge model which is the key threat to capitalism. He sees it, then, as analogous with the collapse of feudalism and the emergence of capitalism itself.

The five principles of transition are:[56]

To understand the limits of human will-power. This is not understood by Leninists — the classic Leninist left-wing parties who thought that volunteerism would be enough to overcome capitalism.

Ecological sustainability. We must change human beings as well as the economy — it's about changing *us* and not just something outside us called "The Economy". That surely echoes Gibson-Graham — that's what a lot of their work is about. You could say that their work is really emphasising that above everything else. And perhaps, to adopt the perspective of the *Manifesto for an Accelerationist Politics*, it's the emphasis on that without the other stuff that perhaps makes it so political.

Attack the problem from all angles. So, again, it requires a kind of diversity, again echoing Gibson-Graham.

Maximise the power of information. I think this is about transparency, knowledge — perhaps linked in with WikiLeaks and all that kind of stuff.

So, his steps towards this would be:[57]

An accurate and open-source computer simulation of current economic reality. He thinks it's possible, because of the computing power that's available now, which was not possible at previous points in history.

A shift to a "wiki-state" model. Switch off the privatization model. Reshape markets towards sustainable, collaborative and socially just outcomes. Make space for collaborative, peer-to-peer and non-profit activities. Force corporations to drive change. Suppress or socialize monopolies. Let market forces disappear. Some markets can survive but it's the difference between market forces and markets, I think — it's quite interesting. And he's saying in energy, in order to reach sustainability, market forces must be suppressed entirely. Socialise the finance system. Pay everyone a basic income — like Nick and Alex — and unleash the network.

OK, just to summarise, then:

Gibson-Graham: economic diversity, and a production of new kinds of subjectivity and affects, that's their emphasis. With Nick and Alex, it's those demands of basic income, automation, reduced working week, universal basic income, the shift to post-work. And with Paul Mason, then, it's this kind of info-knowledge model — a kind of open source politics...

So, what do people think? Having rushed through Mason a bit... I'd just like to hear what people's initial thoughts are...

Rank them! Which is the best? Which is the worst?

STUDENT #9: I don't really have a ranking... (*Laughter.*)

MF: No! That was pathetic, don't really rank them...!

STUDENT #9: When I was reading the text, I was thinking of an article I'd just read about a really trendy leader or CEO of a company, and he said he had a burn-out because he was working in a job where he didn't have any hierarchy, so no one was telling him what to do, and that made him have the burn-out because he was having difficulty self-managing and stuff. And I was just wondering, in relation to the working ethic of "no pain, no gain", what happens if you don't have to work? Would you do the fun Wikipedia stuff, or would people just become really lazy? I don't know, this is just something I wanted to ask.

MF: It's a good question, right? But it's bleak, isn't it?

Isn't Wikipedia already an answer to that? Wikipedia isn't "work" — they don't get paid for it. Two hundred people probably do get paid but most people who contribute to it don't, and aren't working — so that's already an answer to that.

STUDENT #9: Yeah, but now I'm at [university], I've been reading a lot, because I'm forced to read a lot, but also, I like to read a lot when I'm not here. I don't do it because I'm forced to... I don't know — what do you feel? I feel like this is the argument of neoliberalism: once you're in a job you get stuff done — because you have to — so what happens when you're not in that context?

MF: No, no, it is a good question, but the argument is: isn't a lot of cultural production the answer to that? Most culture that's produced is not remunerated — at all, never mind about in a small way.

STUDENT #13: You could argue that it would increase cultural production because everyone would have more time.

MF: Yeah! I think this is good...

STUDENT #14: What about culture produced under different circumstances? I think some of the most amazing things that people write are written because they're suffering from a system that they don't want to be exploited by. So, imagine what would be produced if there was nothing bad out there. (*Laughter.*) The most interesting pieces of culture have always been counterculture, so I'm just thinking: what could a counterculture look like in a post-work society?

MF: OK, this is really interesting, but it does show the influence of this cult of suffering that Nick and Alex talk about: the idea that this suffering isn't crucial. That's one thing [but] that's not necessarily repudiating what you're saying... (*Mark and various students talk over one another.*)

STUDENT #15: ... Maybe there's some kind of resublimation of your capacity to do something else instead, with more time...

MF: Yeah, I mean, we're still faced with mortality, we will still face loss. Work isn't the only form of suffering... Sorry, that sounded a bit sarcastic... But, you know, other forms of suffering would be there. The full Promethean ambition would be to eliminate mortality as well, which the Soviets, at some point, thought would be possible — I mean, why not? What are the limits? This is Prometheanism...

But [student #12] — I think you wanted to say something...

STUDENT #12: I was just going to say — socially, the question of leisure time: you'd have to re-evaluate what that is in the face of post-work things... Like, why would you make stuff? The impetus would be different. There'd be a different drive to it. I don't know, I just keep thinking about that.

MF: I just think about the Beatles. What does a post-work society look like? It kind of looks like what life was like for them, doesn't it? They didn't have to work. They'd made enough money, surely, by the early Sixties to just not work. Then their most interesting, experimental stuff emerged. Their most interesting, experimental stuff emerged partly because they were freed from the pressure of having to worry about salary — they actually sold more anyway!

Is that a silly example or not? Isn't that what haunts us about the Sixties counterculture? It was some indication of what a post-work society was. All of that was made possible by — reinforcing your point — partly, because people got grants to go to art school and the like, and were freed up from the pressures of drudgery for a while...

So, I think we've got some indication of what a post-work society would look like in terms of cultural production but, of course, that doesn't necessary answer your point because that was still in the context of a broader society at work. But, as I say, you think about the Beatles or any successful artist who carries on working and does interesting stuff — aren't they the argument against that? If only their early work was interesting, when immediately freed up from the pressures of work — I think your argument would be valid — but if after a period of time, when they're effectively liberated from the pressures of work, their work — well, is work the right word for what they're producing? — if it continues to be interesting and, in fact, becomes more interesting, doesn't that suggest that you don't need at least that form of suffering...

STUDENT #9: It's interesting because it really points out the myth that creativity can only occur when you're suffering — which, in my opinion, is bullshit...

MF: Well, it might not be a myth...

STUDENT #9: It is for me at least.

MF: It might be a myth, it might not be a myth — but the thing is, it's a bit hard to test it, I think, because we're in a world of suffering, so we don't know what a world without suffering would be like. But we've got some sense of what a world without certain kinds of suffering would be like, because we've seen what happens to certain people when they're released from it.

OK, this is a good start, isn't it? I think it's the kind of thing we want to be thinking about. It directly relates to what Marcuse would want to talk about — these questions...

I'd like every week for someone to introduce the texts — not me. You can introduce it however you like — it doesn't have to be a formal presentation, but just start off talking about them, so it's not me starting off — obviously I've done it today. And I'll probably do something like this for next week as well, just as a sort of back up... Far too much of me talking today, but I think we've ended up in a space for more discussion.

So, would anyone like to volunteer, then, to do Marcuse for next week?

STUDENT #16: I'll do it.

MF: Fantastic! And anyone for Ellen Willis...?

STUDENT #17: I'll do it.

MF: Ah, thank you very much. If you'd like to do handouts or a PowerPoint or whatever, you can do that. Or you can just raise a few points. Whatever you want to do, so you're starting off and not me...

STUDENT #16: Just, like, a few minutes?

MF: Yeah, yeah, yeah, just a few minutes. Yeah. Just, key points — things you want to discuss — etc.

OK, so that's... that's that... That's the first one. (*Laughter.*)

Lecture Two:
"A Social and Psychic Revolution of Almost Inconceivable Magnitude": Countercultural Bohemia as Prefiguration

14 NOVEMBER 2016

(A student begins the session by introducing Marcuse's concept of the dialectic of civilisation, focussing on Sigmund Freud's use of the apocryphal story of the 'primal horde', *first described by Charles Darwin, which Freud discusses in his 1913 book* Totem and Taboo. *It is a fairly long and thorough introduction. For brevity, a brief summary is provided below:*

Freud invokes Darwin's thesis to explain the emergence of the prohibition of incest in society. "Darwin deduced from the habits of the higher apes that men, too, originally lived in comparatively small groups or hordes within which the jealousy of the oldest and strongest male prevented sexual promiscuity", he writes.[1] When the oldest male becomes frail and younger males contest his position, the victor will form a new community and necessarily drive all the other males out. Freud argues, through references to various other anthropologists, that, over time, "this would produce what grew into a conscious law: 'No sexual relations between those who share a common home.'"[2]

Through this shift from social relation to conscious law, the figure of the primal father is substituted by a 'totem'. This totem could be an object real or imagined. In some primitive societies, the sacrifice of the patriarch is transferred to the killing of an animal; in Freud's twentieth-century case studies, the figure of the primal father becomes more symbolic.

Freud folds these various observations into his theory of the Unconscious, and particularly his conception of the Oedipus complex, relating the symbolic form of the primal father to the emergence of the superego. What is key, for Freud, is that the experience of internalising the prohibition of incest constitutes a foundational subjugation — that is, control and repression — of desire in society.

Herbert Marcuse, in his 1955 book Eros & Civilization, *takes these observations a step further, updating them for the times and exploring the extent to which the subjugation of human desire is today enforced through far more pervasive systems of control and for reasons far more complex than the prohibition of incest and the principle of exogamy.*

Following the student's introduction, Fisher places the book in its historical context as well as the wider context of the course.)

MARK FISHER: OK. This is from 1955 then — Marcuse's text. Marcuse himself was a late member of the Frankfurt School, and continues in the spirit of the Frankfurt School, and particularly, I guess, in terms of the overarching project of some kind of fusion of Freud with Marx.

I think there's a difference in tone from Marcuse than his predecessors, perhaps the best known of which is Adorno, and that tone I think is partly to do with the fact that Marcuse is far more a Romantic figure in lots of ways... I don't mean in the everyday sense of "romance" but in the more philosophical and cultural sense. He still places a high value on the importance of art. Adorno does this but, with Adorno, you get very little sense of what life beyond capitalist domination could provide. With

Marcuse, I think you get a much stronger and more vivid sense of that.

I suppose we have to ask the question: why turn to Freud at all? Why is Freud important? And that's a question we can pose to the Frankfurt School and also to ourselves in relation to this course. I suppose, in relation to this module, the answer is that even if we disagree with Freud's account of desire, we have to go round or past it; through it. Of course, part of the significance of Freud was that he made desire central — to his own theories but also to his understanding of the way in which human individual psyches and the social world function.

There's perhaps two ways in which this goes in Freud's work. The first is that quasi-biologistic naturalisation of currently existing desires — so, the rooting back of desires that are now available, or expressed even, to some kind of biological root. "Anatomy is destiny" is the famous quote... But if anatomy is destiny... Well, we can change our anatomies now — that's available in a way it wasn't to previous historical generations. That's perhaps not quite as deterministic as it first appeared — but that would be the conservative side of Freud: biologistic and naturalising.

The other side of Freud, though, is the idea that there is no natural form of desire whatsoever, actually. This is what Marcuse is trying to cling to in Freud — the historical side of Freud's work.

(There is an interruption as students arrive late; a jostling of chairs and voices. Fisher says he will try and request a bigger room for future sessions.)

OK, but I think the radical side of Freud then goes from this other dimension: the idea of the historicity and plasticity of desires — and perhaps the shift from the word "instinct" to the word "drive" is more than a kind of translation issue there... Anyone speak German?... Yeah, so in German it's "Trieb", right? The word... Rather than "instinct", it's more like "drive", I think.

STUDENT #1: I haven't read Freud and I don't know what he uses, but...

STUDENT #2: Sorry, can you repeat the word?

MF: Sorry: T-R-I-E-B... *(There are murmurings of acknowledgement and understanding.)* Yeah... So how would you literally translate that?

STUDENT #3: How is it called again? What you just said?

MF: *Trieb.*

STUDENT #3: Ah, yes!

STUDENT #2: I'd definitely go for "drive" but, as you say, it's not the same...

MF: Yeah! But there's a very different emphasis, isn't there, from "instinct" to "drive". When that translation happens, it's a big decision.

OK, so what is the distinction, do you think? What's at stake? If you say something is a "drive", how is that different to talking about an instinct?

STUDENT #3: "Instinct" is very biological, no?

MF: Right, yes. So, there's a machinic or non-biological nature to "drive", at least in principle, which implies the capacity of redirecting, reformulating drives. And also, the fact they are just not natural. They're not "given" in the biological nature of beings, of humans. I guess there is that one way of separating out human beings from other animals... You could say: "Do animals have drives?"

This is not a rhetorical question, it's an open question. I think we can pose the question "Do animals have drives?" Because we can say they have instincts, but do they have drives? I think we can also pose the reverse: "Do we really have anything *like* an instinct?" And if we do, what is the whole apparatus of Freudian explanation supposed to be doing, in a way? If there are already existing instincts, then why is so much cultural work required in order to... One of the radical implications of Freudian theory is that something like heterosexuality is the achievement of a *massive* process of acculturation — that it doesn't just *occur*, that there has to be a whole series of initiations, channellings, closing down of potential desire, which has to occur in order for something like heterosexuality to be seen as normative...

So, I think that these two kinds of Freud are in conflict, or at least there's a tension between them, and part of the reason Marcuse wants to stick with Freud, instead of just ignoring him as a conservative thinker... Instead of saying that, then, he wants to say, well, no, if we flip it around, we can see Freud, rather, as a thinker of the historicity of desire. This is why we have things like the story of the primal horde.

The story of the primal horde, which you referred to, haunts Freud's texts, most notably *Totem and Taboo* from 1904[3] and *Moses and Monotheism* from... Well, I think it was eventually published in 1939. One of the themes of Freud's work in general, and of those essays in particular, is repetition. The big question of psychoanalysis, you could say, is — "*the* big one": one of the big ones (*laughter*) — is: "Why do we repeat things which are unpleasurable?"

This is the phenomenon that he observes in *Beyond the Pleasure Principle*, and this is the distinction between Freud and a kind of Anglo-Saxon style utilitarianism. You know that the famous slogan of utilitarianism — who's the founder of utilitarianism...?

STUDENT #4: Bentham?

MF: Yeah, Bentham! Yeah, yeah. Simple stuff... It slips... Bentham is the headless mannequin... Or is it his actual body...?

STUDENT #4: It's his body but they've got his head in a box and you can request to see it.

MF: Yeah, which is at UCL?

STUDENT #4: UCL, yeah.[4]

MF: Yeah. That's just bizarre... Whenever I think of Bentham, I think of headless Bentham... Anyway... Bentham famously proclaimed that mankind is at the mercy of two sovereign masters: pleasure and pain. Human beings will pursue pleasure and avoid pain. It seems obvious! But Freud discovers that this apparent truism just doesn't hold up, actually. Much of the time, we will pursue things which seem, on the face of it, painful. There is, in a way, a second-order level of enjoyment, which is the enjoyment of things which, on the first-order level, seem to be painful. And yet, part of the problem that Freud had with his patients was this attachment to a second-order level of enjoyment. Because if it's simply a matter of people being in pain, and that pain was straightforwardly undesirable, then you could fairly easily wean them off the pain, but if there's some second kind of satisfaction to be derived from things which were superficially painful, then it's much more problematic, and other attachments are formed. This is what stood in his way and one of the key things that he finds.

So, then there is this problem of "repetition compulsion", which is central to *Beyond the Pleasure Principle* of 1921. It's commonly known that *Beyond the Pleasure Principle*, like *Civilisation and its Discontents*, was substantially informed by the experience of World War One. Because one of the things that Freud was puzzled by was shellshock, from the First World War. Shellshock, which is a phenomenon whereby people would repeat the trauma of a shell going off near them. So, if a book fell from a shelf, they would immediately be thrown back into the situation of a shell having exploded close to them.

We kind of take this for granted now. Freud asked the naive question: Why? Why do people do this? Because if an organism was simply motivated by staving off panic and moving towards pleasure, then what compels it to repeat these extremely unpleasurable things? Part of the answer for Freud is some kind of mastery over the trauma. The repetition enables the organism to claim the trauma for itself, in a way. And he discusses this with the so-called "fort–da" game... He plays this game [with his grandson], to do with the absence of his mother, who is spending more and more time apart from him, he plays this game which involved, I think, some sort of small object that you throw away and it's here, it's gone, it's there, it's gone, it's here, it's gone... And so, instead of simply avoiding the pain of the absence of his mother, he turned it into a game of which he could have some sort of mastery, and which tells him some sort of narrative in the process.

This compulsion to repeat, then, becomes crucial.

But beneath that there is then this more metaphysical problem that emerges for Freud from the very basic drives of human beings. And this is where he starts to posit the so-called "death drive", which is highly complicated... We'll broach it though.

Partly, it's complicated because Freud himself is not fully sure what he thinks it is. You can see it in almost diametrically opposed ways, in some respects. The first way to see it, then, would be simply as a destructive or aggressive drive, which is simultaneously also the drive towards self-destruction. And Freud starts to posit this as an independent drive from erotic drives, the drives for pleasure. But, hold on a minute ... You see, what he also starts to think is, well, is this really *opposed* to the pleasure principle or another form of the pleasure principle? Because what the death drive ultimately seems to be aiming towards, at least in one of its versions, is acquiescence, peace, ultimate calm — the release from desire itself. This is the so-called "nirvana principle"... We can see it as if the organism is like an elastic band that is being pulled. It's in a state of tension. And there is this innate impulse towards the release of that tension, just in the tension itself. If I keep pulling the elastic band, something doesn't pull it back — it pulls itself.

This is one way that Freud starts to think of the death drive. The death drive has to be pivoted in its aim, and this is how Marcuse essentially discusses it — the erotic drives are there to impede the goal of the death drive towards acquiescence. The organism finds its own way to death — that's the line that he takes.

There's another way of thinking about the death drive. A lot of Lacanians take this view of the death drive. People like Žižek. The death drive doesn't aim at death; it doesn't aim towards a final state of acquiescence. It aims at, rather... I don't want to say an indifference to death.

One of Žižek's examples is *The Red Shoes*. Has anyone seen that?

STUDENT #5: What film?

MF: *The Red Shoes*? Yeah, it's where a ballerina puts on a pair of enchanted dancing shoes and they basically dance her to death. She's initially in a state of ecstasy but, eventually, she can't keep dancing at that sort of frenzied pitch, and so she dies.

The point is not that she was taken over by something which aimed at killing her. It's that she happened to die because the drive made her indifferent to death; indifferent to organic death. This is a drive that was stronger than the desire to avoid death.

So, there are these two almost diametrically opposed senses of the death drive here, but what they have in common is this antipathy towards the idea of a utilitarian-style disposition of our desires. So, there's all this to contend with. And this leads Freud, then, into his most pessimistic theses, which are expressed most powerfully in *Civilisation and its Discontents*, which haunts this chapter of Marcuse's *Eros and Civilisation*.

Civilisation and its Discontents, then... I think you explained this well. *(In reference to the student's introduction.)* The claim of *Civilisation and its Discontents* is that discontent is inherent to civilisation. It's not possible to imagine a civilisation from which discontent has been banished. And you may remember Freud's famous claim that the goal of psychoanalysis was not to eliminate madness, which was impossible...

(The seminar is interrupted again by someone at the door of the classroom, for whom there is no seat available. There is more jostling of chairs.)

Right, so, where were we... *Civilisation and its Discontents*, yeah. So, there is an antagonism between civilisation and pleasure! Why? Well, the idea was, on a simple level, if people were allowed to enjoy themselves, if people were allowed to pursue their pleasure all day, they wouldn't do anything!... Well, they wouldn't do anything except pursue that pleasure! They wouldn't produce the necessities of life. There wouldn't be agriculture. People wouldn't produce dwellings to live in. They wouldn't produce other kinds of goods, which could be enjoyed, or which were simply necessary in order for life to exist. So, actually, it's not even conceivable as a thought experiment, because this kind of repression-free environment is not sustainable — it couldn't sustain itself!

But here is a point that Marcuse picked up. What are the assumptions behind this? What are the assumptions behind the idea that this level of discontent is necessary? The assumption is *scarcity*, fundamentally. That is the fundamental assumption.

Scarcity: the struggle over resources; the fact there is a natural abundance means there must be work. If there is work, then there is someone to do the work. If this work is not, in itself, intrinsically pleasurable or enjoyable then there must be some compulsion towards doing it — a *strong* compulsion which overrides people's more primary desire for pleasure. And so, given that that's all the case, this is the origin of repression, as a response to scarcity. *There is no civilisation without repression.* Repression is the foundation of civilisation. That's it! And that's a tragic tale.

In many ways, if Marcuse is in a lineage of Romantic thinkers, then Freud, I think, fits himself into a lineage of pessimistic thinkers and tragic thinkers. There's no way beyond this, at all. And that's why a lot of Marxist revolutionaries simply reject Freud out of hand, because they say it's just conservative. It's saying utopia is impossible, and it's impossible for quasi-biological reasons. But I think, then, Marcuse is working away at the fact that it *isn't* just biological, *even* on Freud's own account. It *is* historical and it *is* to do with work. And history and work are not fixed and immutable. They are — by their very nature — changeable. And this is what *Eros and Civilisation* brings about, then: it is trying to work through, or work a way out of, the tragic impasse suggested by *Civilisation and its Discontents*.

It's worth thinking again about the role of the *myth* of the primal horde, that you talked about: what role this plays for Freud. A lot of Freud's work at this time is what I call "retro-speculative", in that it was based on *some* kind of anthropology... This idea of the primal horde: he didn't just make it up himself... It's fairly weak, empirically, but its function seems to be, now, and even by Marcuse's time, more a kind of myth of psychoanalysis than something which is believed to have actually happened.

So, why did Freud talk about the primal horde? And why is he interested in it? Well, on both occasions, in *Totem and Taboo* and *Moses and Monotheism*, what Freud is trying to account for is religion. Where does religion come from? Particularly Judeo-Christian religion? I think, as people have pointed out, the hubristic, crazy courage of Freud, when he was in London in flight from the Nazis, writing *Moses and Monotheism*, which, in lots of ways, undermines the very basis of Judeo-Christianity... OK, so what was the argument there? The argument there, in both cases, was to do with the role of the primal father figure, which you talked about.

The primal father figure, as you said, has exclusive or, at least, first claim on basic provisions and access to women. He has the first claim on that. But at some point in history, the brothers — who aren't necessarily biological brothers — the sons — who aren't necessarily biological sons — the father wasn't literally a father; the father was always-already a symbolic function — but nevertheless, at this stage of history or this stage of the myth, the symbolic father and the physical father are one — one entity — which can be destroyed, in theory. So surely *this* would be the point, then, in which repression was done away with — repression under the name of the father. What is this myth about then? It is to say: Where does repression come from? Why do people repress themselves? They are repressed because of the negative father. The father says no. I think it's Foucault who makes the pun "the name of the father" and the "no of the father", which are similar in French: *nom* and *non*.[5]

But the brothers get together and they think, "There's loads of us and there's only one of that fat bastard. *(Laughter.)* Why do we continue to obey these strictures? Why don't we not just overthrow him?" So not only do they overthrow him, they violently kill him, dismember him, and eat him. (I think this is quite central to "Sex, Gender, Species", if people are doing that.[6]) So they eat him. This is the *audacity* of Freud. It's amazing, right? He's saying this is the origin of the communion meal, which is bizarre when you think about it. "This is the body of Christ which was given for you". So, you eat him. Partly, he's trying to say, where would such a myth have come from? He thinks only from some unconscious memory passed down where the father was actually killed and consumed.

OK. So, that's it then! Jubilee! Carnival! Father is dead. No more oppression.

No. Not OK. That's not how it works.

(Laughter.)

What Freud's saying is, at this point, what happens, instead of getting rid of the father, the father becomes eternalised in the form of guilt and remorse. The point at which the sons have killed the father they don't leap around jubilantly. They feel guilty. And the father, from being a finite figure, becomes, then, a kind of virtual spectre who is infinite. You can get away from the physical father, but you can't get away from the introjected voice of the father, which is never satisfied, which is always calling for more, always making demands which can't be met, and which can't now be reasoned with. He probably couldn't be reasoned with before, but he definitely can't be now.

This is the origins of the superego and what Lacanians call the Big Other: the basic form of repressive authority within society. But, what's interesting for Freud, what is also the origin of morality, as such, is the fraternal feelings that the brothers have amongst each other. This is where morality originally comes from. Although there's no literal memory of this — probably because it never happened — even on Freud's account there is no literal memory of this; it's an unconscious memory which is passed down.

The agency of the father, then, is the agency of mortification; the deadening of the flesh. In order to be initiated into society, you have to give up something crucial. You have to give up desire — and, specifically, you could say, this is desire for the mother. Now we're back to the stereotypical core of what people think Freud is about: the idea of desire for the mother. But now I think we can see where this desire for the mother comes from. It isn't that the desire for the mother comes first. Instead, the desire for the mother stands in for some other desire, which is the desire not to exist at all as a separate entity. You've all heard about "separation anxiety": the infant's horror at finding itself to be a finite entity, having to fend for itself in the world. What it's haunted by, then, is a myth — or an image, in the Lacanian sense of the imaginary — of a vague, blurry, dream-like sense of fusion with the mother.

It's one of the things that Deleuze and Guattari say in *Anti-Oedipus*: before there is a sense of a "mother" and a "child", there is no difference between a mother and a child at all. It is this that is most earnestly desired: the annihilation of the individual subject and the return to the state of fusion in the womb. In other words, this is a form of death drive in itself: the annihilation of individual subjectivity, the return to a state of acquiescence, where you could say all desire is met but where also there is no such thing as desire at all. If all your desires are being quenched, then you don't have desire anymore. That relationship between dying and satisfaction is irrelevant.

OK, so that's the big Freudian backstory... So, where does Marcuse come in with this? Partly, as I say, it's to draw out that historical dimension. Again, the stereotype of Freud is about the Oedipal triangle — it's about everyone wants to have sex with their mother. But the question is: why is that the case? Does that provide a full answer? I think, according to Marcuse: no, it isn't the full answer, because it isn't really the sexual or erotic drives that come first. It's the question of work that comes first.

So, why is there repression? There's repression so that people work, so that people can be made to work. This is the fundamental switch that we need to make. He's saying this, then, not so much in that it's opposed to Freud. It's already there in Freud's text but the emphasis is slightly skewed. So, what if people didn't have to work? What if not all work was unpleasant or painful? According to Freud, then, on page 70, which Marcuse paraphrases: "The chain of inhibitions and deflections of instinctual aims cannot be broken".[7] And then a quote from Freud:

"'Our civilisation is, generally speaking, founded on the suppression of instincts'."[8] And Marcuse continues:

> Civilisation is first of all progress in *work* — that is, work for the procurement and augmentation of the necessities of life. This work is normally without satisfaction in itself; to Freud it is unpleasure, painful. In Freud's metapsychology there is no room for an original 'instinct of workmanship'...[9]

Then a little further down the page:

> The basic work in civilisation is non-libidinal, is labor; labor is 'unpleasantness,' and such unpleasantness has to be enforced. 'For what motive would induce man to put his sexual energy to other uses if by any disposal of it he could obtain fully satisfying pleasure? He would never let go of this pleasure and would make no further progress.'[10]

That's, I think, something which we've just said... And on page 72:

> The work that created and enlarged the material basis of civilisation was chiefly labor, alienated labor, painful and miserable — and still is. The performance of such work hardly gratifies *individual* needs and inclinations. It was imposed upon man by brute necessity and brute force...[11]

Now, you'll see there that the two things aren't the same, are they? Brute necessity is one thing; brute force is another. And you can see this sort of doubling in a lot of those key myths such as the myth of the kids killing the primal father. What he seems to say is that the father becomes the fall-guy, in a way, for the fact that you can't attain full libidinal satisfaction.

There's an interesting narrative here if you follow it through. Initially they're thinking, "if only we got rid of the father, then we would be able to get this full enjoyment". But then they find it isn't just down to the father, actually — there's some other intrinsic problem which blocks it. Necessity itself, you could say. It's the nature of the world itself that means we would be unsatisfied. But necessity has to be enforced by domination.

What we're partly seeing, then, is this repeated cycle whereby there is an initial rebellion, the rebellion succeeds to some extent, but ends up reproducing domination. Part of the value of Freudian theory for the Frankfurt School in general, for Marcuse in particular, was that this provides an explanation for why this would be the case. Instead of displacing the father, the rebels *re*place the father and take on the function of the father themselves.

> From the slave revolts in the ancient world to the socialist revolution, the struggle of the oppressed has ended in establishing a new, 'better' system of domination; progress has taken place through an improving chain of control. Each revolution has been the conscious effort to replace one ruling group with another; but each revolution has also released forces that have 'overshot the goal,' that have striven for the abolition of domination and exploitation. The ease with which they have been defeated demands explanations.[12]

He talks about self-defeat, then, as being key to it.

Part of what is happening, then, is — and this is an interesting tension with Willis, who we'll come to shortly — he thinks the family, as you said, has *less* significance than it used to have. Why? Because it's the depersonalisation of the superego.

Just briefly then: the tripartite division which Freud introduces in his later work — between the id, the ego, and the superego — the superego *is* the internalised voice of the father insomuch as it speaks of symbolic limits. Saying no, demanding more of the individual than the individual can ever meet. The superego is the *introjected* forces of social repression but it's not a rational agency. Let's be clear about that. Its demands *cannot be met*. The id, then, would be the entity which sought for more direct satisfaction of desires. And the ego, really, does not exist in and of itself. It exists as the mediation of the tension between those two things.

The superego function is closely associated with the father in older forms of society but then becomes distributed through institutions of administration in contemporary society. And that means that, partly, it's a problem that has been there since the killing of the father figure failed. There's no one to blame — everyone's guilty, but no one is. So, as he says, you just face smiling officials. "Ehh, it's sort of their fault but it's not really because the whole system is a system of constraints and repressions, of which they are themselves victims. They are not the authors of these things".

How do we get out of this? The concept of surplus repression is key, which you touched on. In most imaginable societies, some level of repression is required in order for people to produce anything. But then surplus repression is the additional social repression on top of that, beyond necessity. Beyond quasi-biological necessity, there is also cultural and social pressure.

The key thing for me is scarcity. Modern society really ought to be, in many ways, the most repressive, considering the generalisation of the father function far beyond the father. However, there is the other side to it. Technology, in particular, has produced the conditions for the elimination of scarcity and the removal of drudgery. This is on page 76:

> The excuse of scarcity, which has justified institutionalized repression since its inception, weakens as man's knowledge and control over nature enhances the means for fulfilling human needs with a minimum of toil. The still prevailing impoverishment of vast areas of the world is no longer due chiefly to the poverty of human and natural resources but to the manner in which they are distributed and utilized. This difference may be irrelevant to politics and to politicians, but it is of decisive importance to a theory of civilisation which derives the need for repression from the 'natural' and perpetual disproportion between human desires and the environment in which they must be satisfied. If such a 'natural' condition, and not certain political and social institutions, provides the rationale for repression, then it has become irrational. The culture of industrial civilisation has turned the human organism into an ever more sensitive, differentiated, exchangeable instrument, and has created a social wealth sufficiently great to transform this instrument into an end in itself. The available resources make for a *qualitative* change in the human needs. Rationalization and mechanization of labor tend to reduce the quantum of instinctual energy channelled into toil (alienated labor), thus freeing energy for the attainment of objectives set by the free play of individual faculties. Technology operates against the repressive utilization of energy in so far as it minimizes the time necessary for the production of the necessities of life, thus saving time for the development

of needs *beyond* the realm of necessity and of necessary waste.

But the closer the real possibility of liberating the individual from the constraints once justified by scarcity and immaturity, the greater the need for maintaining and streamlining these constraints lest the established order of domination dissolve. Civilisation has to defend itself against the specter of a world which could be free.[13]

This is Marcuse as a kind of accelerationist! And this carries on on page 80, which is where he sounds the most accelerationist: "What is retrogressive is not mechanization and standardization but their containment, not the universal coordination but its concealment under spurious liberties, choices, and individualities".[14] He continues, after a typical Frankfurt School list of the miserable pleasures of modern society — refrigerators and apartments: "They have innumerable choices, innumerable gadgets which are all of the same sort and keep them occupied and divert their attention from the real issue — which is the awareness that they could both work less and determine their own needs and satisfactions".[15]

Just to summarise: for me this is the core of what is a significant text for this module. Marcuse identifies the long history of dynamics behind the "performance principle" or, as you said, what I think is virtually identical with the "work ethic".[16] He's a kind of Romantic and a Kantian, in lots of ways. He follows the classical lineage of philosophy which is saying: What is freedom? Freedoms are things that are pursued for their own ends, rather than for extrinsic ends, rather than for ends imposed upon us by others. When there is scarcity, we first of all have to deal with that scarcity as a problem. We have to engage with that scarcity. It really has to be dealt with. But when technology can do a lot of that work for us, then that excuse no longer remains. What you have, then, is a sheer amount of surplus repression which is just about maintaining domination for its own sake, and just about retaining the illusion of the impossibility of freedom for human beings, i.e. people being autonomous and working less and determining their own needs and satisfactions.

I hope that some fairly strong links can be seen between this and some of the things we talked about last time, in terms of a post-work society as being central to postcapitalism.

As I said, this is my pitch of considering Marcuse as something of an accelerationist. Isn't the final phrase about pursuing alienation right through? "The elimination of human potentialities from the world of (alienated) labor creates the preconditions for the elimination of labor from the world of human potentialities".[17] A typical Frankfurt School reversal.

OK. So, this is 1954. These ideas circulate — not necessarily directly from Marcuse, but they're around. And the conditions of the 1960s, then, which are precisely where, in large parts of the Western world, scarcity is substantially reduced, certainly for members of what you might call the "bohemian class" — a newly emergent bohemian class. They don't have to work as much. There are periods, particularly in their youth, when they're free of work for substantial periods, and they start to be inspired by this notion that you can both work less and determine your own needs and satisfactions. And this is the basis of the so-called counterculture of the 1960s, in which Ellen Willis was involved.

So perhaps now we can turn to [student #7] to say a few words about what we think is at stake in Ellen Willis's text.

I guess there's a kind of reverse narrative in place here, by putting Willis's text first [in the course reader], which was also not contemporaneous with the counterculture but came afterwards. She wrote in the late Seventies — I think '79: a very significant year. She's already trying to explain what went wrong and why it didn't really work, but I think there's some kind of resonance between her and Marcuse.

STUDENT #7: Yeah, I think, as you just touched upon, she does point towards how, after World War Two, the Fifties and Sixties, that was more of a Golden Era in terms of feminism — especially radical feminism — than the 1970s, which is when she's talking about what she's lived through as a result of conservatism within society and austerity measures.

There's this resurgence of traditional family values and that directly implicates radical feminists and the counterculture because they feel as though there is this interdependency between capitalism and traditional family values.

The counterculture are anti-capitalist and they feel as though [society] is regressing again. And I find it quite interesting, throughout the text, how there are these constant contradictions and obstacles that she faces personally, and that feminism as a sort of totality faces. So, her desire to get married, which she has once had, and which she once again has, [leads to] this internal struggle over [the] morality [of marriage], because being married is buying into this need to be within a patriarchal family society, which is not good for a feminist in the Seventies. And she also discusses people who were involved in their protests, like men who considered themselves to be feminist but only wanted to liberate women to a certain extent. They wanted them to be liberated but still wanted wives. Or, as you were touching upon just then, this "bohemian class" — she was quite critical of them because a lot of bohemians were from middle-class backgrounds, they never felt the struggles that other people in their situation would have done.

I feel like she has also given up in the text. She wants to pursue her ambitions, also on a selfish level, of seeing her feminist ideas follow through and get past this patriarchal society. But I feel like there's a sense that it is impossible to be unbound from a capitalist society, in her opinion.

MF: OK. I think that's partly why I like it. It registers the historical meaning of the end of the 1970s. But what I also like about it... Ellen Willis, by the way, for people who don't know: she was a culture critic and a music writer; she was involved right in the heart of the counterculture itself. But I think she really overturns a lot of the stereotypes about what the counterculture was and what its unachieved ambitions were.

Why do we still care about the 1960s? Why are we *required* to care about the 1960s? Why does it haunt us at the level of iconography and why do its cultural forms persist? I'd say it has something to do with the unrealised desires that were inherent in those forms and to which those forms still speak...? I don't like this phrase "speak to"... That they're still relevant to.

What comes across from this? I think you're right: she sort of has given up. But she's honest about that. She's saying that this was a part of a general mood, which it was, by the time of the 1970s. So, between Marcuse's text and Ellen Willis's text is this attempt to break out — which fails, which *does* fail. And I think her text is important because she identifies some of the reasons that it failed.

But let's go back to what it actually *wanted* then. What the counterculture aimed at was the phrase that I picked up: "a social and psychic revolution of almost inconceivable magnitude".[18] We who came after the 1960s — even though I was born in the 1960s, although too late to comprehend it at that time — we who come after it find it hard to imagine a time when those ambitions seemed to be realistic. What's being registered in this text by this time is the simultaneous and synchronised emergence of capitalist realism and domestic realism, and their co-implication: the idea that there's no alternative to capitalism and there's no alternative to the family either.

I actually think that domestic realism is even more powerful than capitalist realism in today's world. Even when I was at school, in the 1980s, there were fairly serious debates about alternatives to the family. I remember when I taught teenagers, a few years ago, you'd talk about alternatives to the family and they were just horrified by the very thought of it. And the full tragedy of that was, of course, that many of them had come from very difficult family backgrounds. So, they had an idealised idea of the family that didn't fit with their experience of the family at all. And yet that very idealisation implied that they still held up the family as an idea. The countercultural mission to have done with the family really has almost entirely disappeared now as a widespread cultural phenomenon.[19]

I don't distinguish, in a Kantian sense, between the family as a transcendental structure and a family as an empirical fact. The family, as an empirical fact, is under *massive* pressure. As I understand it, particularly in the UK — I don't know what the figures are worldwide

— but there are more people living on their own than ever before. Of course, divorce has increased beyond all proportion since the 1970s. So, the family is not empirically strong, I would say — it's empirically weak but it is transcendentally strong. It's strong as a sort of basic structure that is still normative. Now if you think of people living collectively, you think of that as a temporary phase, when actually there is more of that than there was in the 1970s, all because people can't afford to live on their own, particularly in London.

So, there's increasing amounts of people living outside the family structure, and yet the family remains normative, I would suggest. You could also note that there are also increasing options for women but none of those options are allowed — none of those options are socially permissible, at least as far as still-dominant right-wing narratives go. If you have a child and stay at home to look after that child, then you're a slacker who should be working. If you don't have a child, then you're free; you're denying nature. *Everyone wants a child, don't they... We know all women do, really...* These things ought to be completely archaic by now. But they're not, are they? And this kind of double bind, which means you've got two contradictory commands at any one time, is key to contemporary forms of subjugation and the continued subjugation of women. Women's magazines are full of these two contradictory commands at any one time. *Love your body! Be who you want to be! Here's a diet... (Laughter.)* This is a long way from what people thought was realistic.

People thought it was realistic. This is what Willis is pointing to. It *was* realistic. We'll get rid of the family and we'll do it *now*. We'll do it now. We'll start living in communes and that'll be it, that's the end of it. But obviously that was ridiculous. But it didn't seem ridiculous at the time! And that's the value of the text

— to bring those two things together. By the end of the 1970s, the Promethean ambition that *this could be undone* — that has disappeared by then, together with this vivid conviction that it could be done.

So, she says there are a number of things that point to why it failed. What were they? What were the main reasons?

STUDENT #8: Is one of the things to do with that idea of how marriage as an institution represses desire because you're going against the idea of instinctive action, in going into some sort of agreement that is long-term and sets up a sort of construct that won't allow, traditionally, for you to follow your desire as it changes?

MF: Yeah, that's part of it. She's suggesting that there's just an inherent conflict between love-relations that shift over time and the permanency of the institution of marriage. And in Nick [Srnicek] and Alex [Williams]'s text they point this out: the more that women have economic independence, the more the idea of something like Universal Basic Income will be respected.[20] There's this yoking of an erotic and emotional set of desires with institutional elements. But why wouldn't that work against marriage? Why wouldn't that work towards living communally? That's a problem. That's why marriages are bad. Therefore, let's all go live in communes instead...

Has anyone lived in a commune? *(No response.)* Even twenty years ago, I reckon there would probably be some people in this room who would have tried it.

It points us towards the privatisation of money, doesn't it? The idea seems to make sense that you share money with your family, but sharing money with people who aren't your family on a permanent basis... Also, collective child-rearing. I know Big Flame, who were a kind of libertarian communist group in the 1970s, did this.[21] They experimented with collective child-rearing. And I think, of course it would work! It's got to work better, doesn't it? It's got to work better than child-rearing within the context of the so-called nuclear family.

You could say the nuclear family has been in crisis since the moment it emerged. Because the nuclear family is new — historically, very new — although it assumes like this quasi-transcendental normativity. Mummy-daddy-me.[22] This is clearly the basis of Freud's model but, of course, it wasn't mummy-daddy-me in Freud's day. It was probably mummy-daddy-nanny-me... Because extended families were the norm throughout much of history, and only recently, under pressure of capitalism, did the nuclear family emerge.

You shouldn't be nostalgic for the extended family. There's lots of problems with it. But you can be nostalgic about certain aspects of it, by comparison to the nuclear family...

It's just by odds, isn't it? If you have a bigger group of people involved in child-rearing, the odds of it going badly wrong or of very specific neuroses being passed on are surely much less?

But the reality of these communes, certainly as they developed in the 1960s... Have people seen that Adam Curtis series? Some of you will have seen it. The *Machines of Loving Grace* thing, where he mocks the commune thing quite heavily.[23] It's probably justified as well...

For me the key thing that she points to is impatience. Impatience, material privilege, and age — which is another form of privilege, in a sense, although not so much now... Impatience, first of all: they thought they could get rid of this straight away. That's crazy. Things that, she said, had lasted thousands of years and we'll get rid of them in a generation no problem. *How do we do it? We'll just go live in a house together and work it out.* But they just didn't have the persistence that families did. They didn't find a way of making this stick over time. So even relatively successful communes only lasted a few years. To think that people hate their own families! It's just not that common. Even if that is the case, nevertheless they still retain some identification with them, probably for the rest of their lives. It shows the power of a deeply embedded family structure, and so I think what she's pointing to is the tenacity of those structures, which aren't just susceptible to voluntaristically being overcome. And she said they meet real needs; the family meets real needs. They might meet them badly... Because the time of Willis is also the time in which the family is under attack from people like R.D. Laing, David Cooper, saying it's the source of mental illness. It's a kind of neurosis and psychosis factory: the family.[24]

People weren't saying that so much by the time she wrote this though, but certainly in the 1960s that was certainly around.

So, impatience, that's the first thing. Impatience. Structures of this tenacity, this length of time, and which are clearly fulfilling some need and, even if they're not, still command a certain level of attachment from that sheer, gross persistence. They are difficult to overcome, if not impossible to overcome entirely.

The second thing she's saying is youth. A lot of people involved in communes were young. They could afford to have these sorts of experiments for a while but, as they got older, they retreated back into the standard structures of Western society.

The other thing she says is wealth and privilege. Most people didn't have the capacity to "drop out". This was obviously key to it, as she points out, and as we see in Marcuse. Relative prosperity is key; the relative prosperity of the US at that time. But that prosperity was not evenly distributed and those who dropped out tended to be those who could afford to do so because, at some level — I'm not saying they were insincere and thought: "Yeah, I can drop out for a while but in a few years I'll be able to drop back in when I have more of a capacity to do so". Nevertheless, they didn't have that base level of anxieties about the risks of leaving behind conservative structures.

This leaves us with a fairly bleak picture... But that's not what I really wanted from this... *(Laughs.)* So, what if we reframe what was happening in the 1960s not as some Golden Era where everything was great and then all went wrong? Willis's analysis gives us some of the resources to think of this as a stalled project. If impatience was a problem, then patience is needed. So how do we develop patience? How do we develop patience sufficient to overcome these very deep and very long-lasting structures? How do we spread out the accessibility of these kinds of experiments of alternative living from particular groups: from youth and from the relatively privileged? And to return to Marcuse: isn't it the case that there's more *real* scarcity now than there was in the 1960s? "Real" is a problematic term...

What are the actual limits? That's a big question. What are the actual necessities now that put limits on human freedom? You won't get a bigger question than that today. Promise.

STUDENT #9: Shelter, food, resources... And I guess the climate is becoming one?

MF: Yeah. This is a bit like Maslow's "Hierarchy of Needs", isn't it...[25] But surely emotional needs must count as equally significant. If all those needs are met but there's no care for each other.

STUDENT #8: One of the quotes that I thought was really interesting was on page 161 where she says:

> The difference has to do with home being the place where when you have to go there they have to take you in — and also being ... something you don't deserve. I have friends who would take me in, but on some level I think I have to deserve them.[26]

And that idea of [the family] being this unit that reinstates that individualism versus a community where you all equally rely on each other and you earn it.

MF: Yeah, but is "community" the right term for it? I have a lot of problems with the term "community", largely because of the way it's been easily appropriated by the right. But also, because it implies an in and an out. Some are in the community and some are out of it. I had a slogan once: "Care without community". Isn't that what we want? Where you can give people the care regardless of whether they belong to the community.

We haven't spoken about the events of last week yet.[27] But isn't that exactly what this new form of right-wing reaction is about — the exact opposite of that. It's restricting care only to a defined community. So, you're literally putting up walls... It's a fantasy.

Something like the NHS, as it was, cared for anybody. So, there's an opposition between the notion of the "public" and the notion of "community". Couldn't we think of them differently? A lot of people talk about "the commons" and all of that, coming from Autonomia and [Antonio] Negri... But isn't the public different again from both the commons and the community? Public health, public good... I think it's different to the commons. Because the commons have this quasi-naturalistic quality about them, which is probably where it comes from — from common land — whereas the public has to be curated, created, cultivated...

We can compare communes with these equally failed attempts within the Soviet system for communal living, for living outside of private space. We can also think about the ways in which basic architecture and housing reinforce this domestic realism of families and individuals, and relegate the notion of living collectively to certain periods of life. Because living in a family *is* living collectively. It's just a very restricted form of it. Isn't part of the function of the family for capitalism that it can contain the desires for collectivity that we have? It's a desire that can only be met by collective groups that is expressed in a form that is often chauvinistic, that is competitive, that is defined by its exclusions as much by its inclusions.

STUDENT #9: Could you say that, as the revolutions against capitalism have failed... As Marcuse says, the surplus repression increased each time, and so, with the counterrevolution, in the new generation we have taken on the guilt of its failure.

MF: Yeah!

STUDENT #9: Almost like they tried to eat the father but didn't succeed and then the father basically financialised their ideas, and then said to us, oh you can have these ideas if you work, and it proves that you can have them without doing this, but you could work loads and then have this existence of no work, or leisure. These things are all subordinated and taken on by capitalism...

MF: Yeah, incorporated...

STUDENT #9: ... And we feel the guilt of the past failures in the fact that, like Marcuse says, if we go to try and start a revolution it'll be beyond reward and redemption. So, we're always watched by our nuclear family. We're leaving behind people that are still going to be suffering because we've watched revolutions happen that aren't inclusive... It's almost like there's two guilts going on. Guilt of the past but also a guilt of the fact that if we were going to succeed in this revolution, they wouldn't come with us. It would never happen that way. We've been taught that we can have parts of these revolutions but only through capital.

MF: Right, so that's partly a Luc Boltanski and Eve Chiapello argument in *The New Spirit of Capitalism*.[28] Capitalism incorporates previous rebellions, particularly creative and artistic rebellion, and then sells it back as this new spirit of capitalism. That's part of what was involved in the Apple commercial.[29] It's no longer grey corporate drones — it's sitting around in hammocks, eating sweets, riding little tricycles around the office and all that sort of thing. Work itself can be creative, etc. etc.

But I think the thing we can say is that this rings ever truer: the line about the spectre of a world which could be free. The spectre of a world which could be free is both further away now — certainly seems further away than it was in the 1960s and the 1970s — the 1970s wasn't immediately a period of decline and reaction, as we'll see when we look at the texts in the fourth week — loads of stuff exploded in the early 1970s in particular — and yet, culturally and politically, existentially, it does seem a lot further away, and that is partly because of things like the fusion of precarity and technology; the production of artificial scarcity. Almost everyone is subject to an artificial scarcity of time: the sense that there is no time to do anything. So, technology, rather than liberating time, particularly communicative technology, has exacerbated and intensified the sense that there is no time in its production of artificial scarcity.

We can see, from Marcuse's perspective, that this isn't an accident. It's not that we're just failing; we could live a life with far less work, but things haven't worked out that way. It's a deliberate strategy at the level of capital and human consciousness, to keep inhibiting and obstructing that possibility: of working less and determining your own needs. It's not a *material* problem. It's a political problem. Even though the material problem is still very severe.

Right, I've had enough of that one...

Who'd like to take on Lukács for the next one? *(No response.)*

I'm not going to say Lukács is easy, but just drag out a few of his concepts...

Please somebody volunteer.

(Student responds inaudibly.)

Ah, thank you.

STUDENT #10: No, sorry, I said I'm not here.

MF: Oh. *(Laughter.)* I was deliberately mishearing there.

STUDENT #11: I'll do it.

MF: OK. You'll do it. Thank you.

I find Lukács really intensely irritating. Just see what you can get out of that.

Nancy Hartsock: a lot easier to read. Anyone want to do that one, on "Feminist Standpoint" theory?

(General murmuring. Two students volunteer and decide who will take on the text amongst themselves.)

OK. So, the issue next week is consciousness and the formation of what Lukács calls "class consciousness" and what I call "group consciousness"...

Thanks everybody.

Lecture Three:
From Class Consciousness to Group Consciousness

21 NOVEMBER 2016

(Student presentation. They take great care to summarise the argument of Lukács' text but struggle to briefly give a theoretical account of its various twists and turns.)

MARK FISHER: Don't worry. Don't worry. It's hard. It's really hard. Just start at a simple level: what is the basic point of what he's trying to argue in this text? What is it about?

STUDENT #1: The quantitative gains of the capitalist system need to be translated into a qualitative change for the proletariat — a move towards not only a form of class consciousness but social possibilities, freedom, and possibilities for social change.

MF: OK. Let's go to basics here. Who was familiar with Lukács at all here before reading this? Anybody? *(Silence.)* OK. Who's familiar with Hegel?... *(Murmuring.)* OK, a bit. Who's familiar with Marx? *(Some slightly more affirmative muttering.)* OK, that's a start.

Look, this is deep-cooked in Hegel. That's why it's infuriating to read. Hegel and Heidegger made it their business to... It's like a sign of a high-quality commodity in their eyes, that it's extremely difficult to read. The

Hegelian influence is very strong in this text, which is why it's stylistically difficult, but it is valuable. I think it's extremely valuable once we get to grips with this.

It's trippy as well. It tries to conceal this, almost, through this ponderous Hegelian system, but it's *extremely* trippy what he's talking about, partly because it is about consciousness.

Why this is valuable, I think — and as I said in the e-mail I sent out to people — I think it's easier to understand it once you've read the Hartsock text; [it's easier to understand] what's at stake in this. Because she's strongly influenced by this text, and what she did in "A Feminist Standpoint" was translating — she's done more than that but at a crude level — she's translating Lukács' arguments from class to gender. In developing it, she develops this idea of standpoints, which she and others then contribute to something called "standpoint epistemology", which is *mind-blowing*, I think. It is mind-blowing. It did blow my mind when I first heard this theory.

It's interesting. It's been around for a long time. [It was published] more than thirty years ago — more like forty since the theory has developed — but it's still little known: standpoint epistemology, in lots of ways. I noticed David Graeber, in his last book — it's a really good book on bureaucracy — he mentions, at the end, standpoint epistemology, saying: "Oh yeah, much of what I've been arguing in this book can be summed up, I've learned, by standpoint epistemology, of which I was not aware". It's interesting, I think, why that is...

(*A student interrupts to ask the name of Graeber's book.*)

The book by David Graeber? It's called *The Utopia of Rules*.[1] Yeah, he mentions standpoint epistemology at the end.

I think it's highly important because it's a really

explosive theory, which breaks with a lot of the key dualisms which still operate in what we still have to call "postmodern thought", where you either have objective truth — which is defined in some naive way — or you have relativism: nothing is really true; nothing is true at all. So you have po-faced Anglo-Saxon empiricists, saying things are what they are, roast beef, that sort of thing[2] — or you have, in the other stereotype, Continentalists who have to complicate everything and say that nothing is fixed or stable and you can't assign determinate meaning to anything... Standpoint epistemology really breaks with both of those positions. It's saying, there are different points of view, but some are better than others.

The standpoint *is different from a point of view*, we should say, first of all. And this relates, straight away, to this complicated question of consciousness. I think most of you are somewhat familiar with Marx. One of Marx's key emphases is on the primacy of the material — something that Nancy Hartsock talks about. The primacy of the material over the idea. The primacy, in other words, of *practice* over mental conceptions. Sometimes that primacy is viewed as more than a primacy but actually as causal. The material *causes* mental conceptions. That's complicated on lots of levels — complicated and controversial within the history of Marxism: how we think of this relation between mental conceptions and, more broadly, culture and materiality. The material doesn't *only* mean physical things; it also means practice.

Right... I've put too many parentheses in, and I've lost myself...

OK. With that emphasis on the primacy of the practice and the material, it might seem that consciousness lies on the side of the idea. Consciousness surely must be a mental conception, must be an idea, and Marx thought the materialist revolution was to bang things on the head, and put matter and praxis first, and ideas second. But what is meant by consciousness, in this sense? What is meant by class consciousness? It is not the same as ordinary phenomenological consciousness.

All of this is embedded in the point of the standpoint — I remember now! The standpoint is not a point of view.

We can all have points of view. And we all do have them. They're already there. But a standpoint has to be constructed by practice. And the easy way to see this, I think, is by the concept of consciousness raising. This was, in a way, what Nancy Hartsock was trying to codify in her theory of standpoint epistemology: the practice of consciousness raising.

Anyone want to describe what consciousness raising is? How does it work?

(*Silence.*)

Alright. (*Laughs.*) Well, it's a powerful, molecular process, I would argue. It is really necessary for any group consciousness to develop. It was developed by feminists — I don't know when it started, to be honest — but it was certainly very prevalent by the time of the Seventies as a strategy. And the power of it is the simplicity of it, partly. All you need is the members of the group together, and when they talk together, honestly and openly, they'll start to see that they have common problems and common interests, and also that the cause of those problems is not them but is something else. Simply *it's not me, it's patriarchy* would be the revelation. *I don't clean the house enough; I always feel bad for not doing that.* Well, the problem is not that you haven't cleaned the house enough. The problem is the set of expectations around that kind of work — the gendering, that kind of thing — which then become denaturalised.

This is what Lukács meant by the "problem of

immediacy". The problem of immediacy is that it is reifying, which is one of the big concepts of Lukács. What's meant by reification? Anyone want to have another go?

(Session is interrupted by a number of late arrivals — Mark comments on also having difficulty in finding the room himself; a new and larger room acquired following the overcrowding of the previous lecture. He also comments on how nice it is.)

Where was I?

STUDENT #1: Were you going to talk about the thing-in-itself?

MF: Right, yeah. OK: reification. What does it mean: reification?

STUDENT #2: *Thing*-ification?

MF: Yeah! Fairly literally: thingification.

One of the themes you'll have noticed running through this — through Lukács' work and this text in particular — is a common philosophical theme of *becoming* versus *being*; the idea that ideology reifies. Ideology turns what is always a process of becoming — which is open-ended and therefore changeable — into something that is fixed and permanent. That's what reification is. And, of course, that's crucial. That's the very purpose of ideology. The very purpose of ideology is to close off the possibility that anything could be different. That's the A–Z of ideology, in fact. But, of course, the second step of ideology is to make itself disappear. Ideology doesn't arrive and say, "I am ideology". Ideology says: "I am nature, and this is how things are". It probably doesn't speak, but even in my metaphor it doesn't really have to say anything. It's *we* who must think in response to it. *This is how things are. They can't be any different.*

I think we have the basic contours in place now, of what's at stake there, which is reification, the fixed product of ideology — naturalisation, on the one hand; on the other hand, consciousness. But consciousness is only developed via practice, so that consciousness raising, to come back to that... What's the difference between consciousness raising and simply knowing something?

STUDENT #3: (*Inaudible comment.*)

MF: Yeah but, paradoxically, the objective level is the level of relations, not the level of things. That's what he's always suggesting.

That's the thing that I think is odd for us today: the confidence with which Lukács — and still Hartsock — will use the terms "science" and "knowledge". It's confident. This is not a pure relativism. As I was saying before, it's neither a relativism nor is it the old view of an objective truth that is already out there lying waiting for us.

The other key concept of Lukács: *totality!* Our friend totality. "Totality" just means the whole system. You can't understand any bit of a system without understanding the whole system, and the whole system is not *a thing* — it's a set of relations. This is why immediacy is such a problem. Immediacy is inherently ideological, and ideologically mystifying. Because the totality is not given in immediacy!

Just look at it this way: part of the difficulty you could say people have is, when they're struggling against things... Patriarchy is not going to come in here and announce itself, any more than ideology is. It's a bit like when Thatcher says that "there's no such thing as society".[3] It's the same sort of claim, because, OK, well, you can't see it, can you? It's not given in immediacy, this society. So, when Lukács talks about the bourgeoisie and a thought mired in immediacy, that's exactly it! The English: we take this to an absurd degree. Things are only what they are and no more, and probably a little bit less. Capitalism itself is not given in experience! You have to construct it in consciousness. It isn't given to you. Your *work* is given to you. *What you do* is given to you. *Your little bit* is given to you. The totality is not given to you in experience. Never. Never! Your experience is only your experience — and not even that. It doesn't belong to you because both you and your experience are already ideologically packaged. That's what I meant: it's trippy quite quickly. This is what he's saying. And that's also why a standpoint is not a point of view. A standpoint is constructed by consciousness and not given in immediacy.

Then it gets even more psychedelic.

Part of the problem of the old idea of objective truth, you could say, was its idea that consciousness has no effect on the truth. That might well be true of the state of a black hole or something like that, but it can't possibly be true of social relations. I'm *in* those social relations! I'm *already* in those social relations. So, when *I* — and it can't be me alone, ever, who does this — when group consciousness develops, when class consciousness develops, when any subordinated group [consciousness] develops, this immediately changes things — straight away. Because in being lifted out of experience, you're broken out of ideology. You — and I'm using this as a second-person plural — *you can then* achieve agency! You can't achieve it before.

Even before you do anything, something has happened, which is the production of this new consciousness. When we think about this set of social relations... Something has shifted in the set of social relations by the sheer fact that your consciousness has shifted anyway. That's the first thing. It's already changed things. Secondly, then, once a group recognises its common interests, then it can act together. Once workers realise the problem is capital, not them — once they stop competing against one another and realise they have a common enemy — capital — this is when they're going to have agency. Similarly, when women realise the problem is patriarchy, not them as individuals, then their consciousness has immediately shifted. *You feel better!* That's the first thing. You'll feel relief from the guilt and misery of having to take responsibility for your own life, which you shouldn't have to — despite everything neoliberal propaganda tells us. *It is not you!* It's a direct inversion of Thatcher! "There's no such thing as society. There are only individuals and their families". It's the other way round! There's no such thing as the individual. But the individual *is* immediately given. And that's part of the problem of immediacy.

STUDENT #4: I have a question.

MF: Yes, please.

STUDENT #4: I think it's very interesting but I'm just trying to get my head around it.

MF: Yeah, of course.

STUDENT #4: Could you then say that, in the terms you talk about the totality and the standpoint, that the standpoint and the realisation of consciousness that goes along with it, is in some way found in this group's position within the whole totality of capitalism? Thinking this in spatial terms now...

MF: Yes! Yeah.

STUDENT #4: OK. I'm thinking of Fredric Jameson and cognitive mapping...[4]

MF: Yes! Yes! Jameson has written extensively on Lukács and cognitive mapping is a direct application of this stuff. Exactly.

But, of course, then, that double thing immediately happens. As soon as they realise their position, they change it. Because they've de-reified it!

STUDENT #4: Right, that would be my next question: what Lukács is saying, then, is that this is always-already a new reification — in finding your position, as he describes it, *being* then becomes very frozen — so I was wondering if, for Lukács, then, if the metaphor of the map would be the problem in itself as it always again suggests a process of reification?

MF: OK. Those are good points. What is the difference between mapping and a map, though? Mapping would not presuppose a map, necessarily. That sounds more like Sartre... This is the kind of thing that he got into with the *Critique of Dialectical Reason* — which I haven't read, but few have, to be fair. Have you seen it? It's about that big... He wrote it on speed. Yeah. And you know what happens when people write on speed! (*Laughter.*) They think it's brilliant... (*More laughter.*) Others... (*Mark trails off and laughs too.*) But no, there's a real problem that Sartre takes on which is this one: what happens when the group, in becoming — and this was influential on Deleuze and Guattari as well — the group, in becoming, it comes together and overthrows the old order. Hold on! It then becomes reified; becomes a thing.

I don't know if Lukács is so much troubled by that... But I wouldn't say I'm an overall expert on his work... So maybe...

But the standpoint is not a thing, though. It's a form of consciousness, you could say.

You see yourself as a member of the proletariat — or, in Hartsock, you see yourself as a woman. You don't see yourself as an individual in that way. But this is hard work. Part of the reason that it's not *a thing*... You can't really reify it because it's a practice. In order to see yourself like that, it's hard work, and it requires a lot of sustaining. That's partly why consciousness-raising is not necessarily the same as knowing something. I might well know that I'm a worker, or I might well know that I'm a woman oppressed by patriarchy, but it's different being able to constantly act on that knowledge, or to act in terms of that knowledge, because all of the other pressures coming from immediacy are going in the other direction. They're saying: *You're an individual. These things don't really exist, do they? Abstractions? Patriarchy? Capitalism? Look, see, what's that over there. That's a table. You can see that. That's real. Other people are there. You can see them. They're real. This other thing isn't really, is it?* You've got this nagging... This is the background noise of ordinary phenomenological consciousness — at least in most societies; certainly capitalist societies.

So, the task of creating a different sort of consciousness that could persist, when you're always thinking in those other terms, at least in the first instance... The point — for Lukács, anyway; I don't know if Hartsock thinks in the same way; I don't know if she's a gender abolitionist — but Lukács is a class abolitionist. And this is one of the paradoxical things that he's pointing to: that class is not given in immediacy in a capitalist society, first of all. Step one: there is no such thing as class. It just isn't there. There are just individuals — some have made more money than others. This is the point of difference between a capitalist system and feudalism. No-one could argue in feudalism that people got where they were because they deserved it, or because of hard work. You couldn't argue that. No-one even thought about it in that way. Hard work was for plebs anyway! Your place in the social hierarchy was symbolically fixed. In other words, it was acknowledged — in the eyes of what Lacan would call the Big Other — it was acknowledged that there was a social hierarchy and positions within that. That's what it was to be a feudal society. Capitalism says there isn't any of that. There are only individuals confronting one another. Some have done better than others. Then we hear the whole other side that is packed into that. Some have done better than others because they've worked harder than others. *If you want to do that well, you should work hard too.*

What is denied in that — it's a fundamental split — there is a fundamental split between groups, and in classical Marxist theory the distinction between — well, how does the distinction go? How do we define the two great classes? What defines the bourgeoisie?

STUDENT #5: Possession of the means of production?

MF: Yeah. That's one of the reasons why this has become problematic in today's world. What is production now? And what is ownership? It was much clearer when Marx said that, right? You owned a factory. You own a factory, so what are you trying to do? You've put some money into that factory and part of that money goes to the hardware, the machinery of the factory, and part of it goes to the workers. But they're essentially the same, aren't they? Paying for workers and paying for machinery is not that different. What are you trying to do? You're simply trying to make more money than you put in. If it doesn't, it's not capital. More money must come out than has gone in.

And part of what Marx is saying is that — I've slightly gone off on a tangent — but the bourgeoisie think that they are the agents of this process. They are what makes things happen. But you could say that capital is more real than they are. This is what I was saying: now, in contemporary society, capital is more real than you are. But in immediacy, it seems the opposite. You're more real than capital. What could be more solid than you? And immediacy will always be that way, because that's what immediacy is!

This is the same for the bourgeoisie. [The problem of immediacy] is why they don't know! They are the puppets of this process, you could say. From their point of view, they're putting more money in, they're making more money. From capital's point of view, they're just the means by which it grows. And this process is, in principle, infinite. And has to be — there always has to be more. This is in the nature of capitalism. Because capital is not money. It's not like cash in your pocket. Capital is money meant to make more money; cash in your pocket is not. It could — you might use it to bet with, or something like that — but when you have the cash in your pocket it's because you're going to spend it. The way capitalists spend money is not the same as you or I buying a coffee, because of the speculative dimension — the investment dimension. You're spending that money so that more money can be made. And there's no end to that process. There can't be.

From the point of view of capital, then — capital is certainly an ideological construction, but it's less ideological than you are — the human bourgeoisie are just a means of its being produced. The big Hegelian story, in this respect, is of human potentiality, of human production being split off... The products of human activity are being split off from the humans who produced them, and coming back as a quasi-autonomous force. It might sound complicated, but it's fairly simple, isn't it? What is the economy if not that? If the economy — just the biggest reification of all, but nevertheless a real thing, at a certain level of reality — the point is that reification produces real effects. Nobody — including and especially capitalists — can will the financial crisis of 2008 away, and yet, absent human beings from the picture, there is no financial crisis. It is entirely an affair of human consciousness, the economy, in that sense, and yet humans have no power to effect it. It's like weather — the economy is like weather. There are people who can be experts in what the weather is going to be and profit from it, but they can't change the weather. Not on a fundamental level. This is part of what's being pointed to: it's fundamental.

But what is capitalism? Capitalism, then, would be this system whereby this alienation — to use that term — of human capacities is taken to its absolute limit. It's a monstrously, prodigiously productive system, yet it's also one which seems to — and *does* — exploit and oppress the majority of the population, and which even the minority have limited capacity to alter.

So, partly then, what this narrative is about is the developing of consciousness. The bourgeoisie cannot have consciousness. They can't see how things really are. This is part of what I think is important about what is being said here. The proletarian does not, by virtue of their being proletarian alone, see the true nature of things. Only by virtue of what we can call consciousness raising — this term was not available to Lukács — only by a process of consciousness raising, by a practice of consciousness raising, can they achieve that. You can't write it off as an empirical and sociological thing. It's about capacities. It's about potential. The proletariat has the potential to grasp the totality. The bourgeoisie lacks that potential because it's too mired in ideology. Why is it mired in ideology? Partly because its experience is not discontinuous. OK, what do I mean by that? Well, it generates the ideology. It generates it, so it lives inside it.

If you're in a subordinated group, you see the way things are talked about by the dominant group, and you see the reality of your life, and you see that they don't match up. Ordinarily, before your consciousness has been raised, you will treat the mismatching of your experience from ideology as a failure in you. *You must have thought of it wrong. You mustn't be thinking about it in the right way.* After consciousness raising, you can see: of course, it's not going to match up. There are two fundamentally different ways of being in the world. There are the ways of the dominant group and the ways of the subordinate group. But precisely because the dominant group dominates, it can't see that. Because it lives inside its own structure of dominance. Whereas, because the subordinated group is subordinated, it has the potential to see the schism.

STUDENT #6: If the dominant group is stuck in a capitalist society, then for whose gain is it ultimately?

MF: Is what?

STUDENT #6: Capitalism.

MF: Well, exactly!

STUDENT #6: I know that's kind of the point, but...

MF: No, that *is* the point! I don't know if Lukács would see it that way, but I certainly see it that way. I think most Marxists saw it that way. That's what I mean [when I say] capital *is* the driver! Capital is purposiveness without purpose. Endless driving... There's no final purpose to it. There's no end point to it, in itself, which I think brings us very close to the core theme of this module, in a way. Because you could say that makes it flat with the structure of desire in itself.

STUDENT #6: Because we're so stuck in it that it feels like there's no way out at all? Because if the most dominant people in our society can't even see it...

MF: You've got to distinguish between empirical power and knowledge. Their very empirical power means that they lack the capacity to develop knowledge. Subordination of the subordinated group gives [that group] the potential to develop knowledge. Knowledge can become the basis for agency; agency can really change things. So only the subordinated have the potential to really change things. The dominated are dominated themselves by their own ideology. They're inside a dream from which they cannot awake.

I think there's a good example in the Nancy Hartsock piece about cleaning the toilet.[5] In that scenario, the men, who are walking around with their highfalutin ideas about X, Y, and Z, they're completely ignorant of the reality of cleaning the toilet and what that means, which is a kind of metonym for all immersion in materiality, or anything that operates as the basis for sociality as such — that is, the social reproduction of humans.

In a way, you could say that access to the lowest level of the materiality of things gives you the potential to have more knowledge of the totality — to come back to that. Because you're in the totality. The dominant group will just float by and not really notice you that much — that's part of the reason they themselves don't see the totality.

STUDENT #7: (*Largely inaudible question that seems to be about how social mobility impacts a view of the totality.*)

MF: I don't think it means you can't move from one [class] to the other. The thing is: what is it to be in a class? I think it's a lot harder to move than people think, for one, and two — I don't know what two was... (*Laughter.*) But this is a very important question and touches on lots of things.

STUDENT #8: (*Another largely inaudible question that seems to be about how class consciousness works and if it is possible for the working class to disappear either when class consciousness is fully uprooted or, alternatively, becomes universally held.*)

MF: OK. These are really important questions, and I think they're related. I'll come back to this first question about moving between classes. (*General chatter.*) Yeah, they are related. I think they are related.

Moving between classes: why it's not that easy to do it. One: it's about, in Kantian terms, what your transcendental assumptions are. In other words, the things that you take for granted and don't really think about at all. If you're in the upper class, you have those certain expectations — they've been bred into you. You've been taught that way. You've been schooled that way. Your home environment tells you: you are that kind of person. Can you ever lose that? Can you *ever* lose that? I don't know if anyone ever has fantasies about this — I know I do — about getting very powerful people sent to jail. Even if they get sent to jail, they'll be fine. Because that sense of entitlement will persist. That sense of entitlement will persist regardless of what happens to them. Do you know what I mean?

I think I've gone beyond Lukács here.

Do it the other way round. The greatest English novels are about this. [Charles Dickens'] *Great Expectations*: one of the great novels about class, I think.

OK. *Great Expectations*: you all know the story here. Or maybe you won't... Ah, I don't want to spoil it for you. (*Laughter.*) OK, so Pip, who is brought up by a common blacksmith, and who is one day taken to the house of a very rich woman to plough in front of her, and is subjected to the gaze and judgement of this woman's ward, a young girl called Estella. As soon as this happens, Pip becomes ashamed of himself. It's just unbearable. He had not realised that he had common boots. He didn't know that. But when he's gone to Miss Havisham's house and seen Estella, she's told him. "Why do you call Jacks knaves? Why do you talk that way?"[6] After that, he's ashamed! It's the difference between self-consciousness — extreme, acute self-consciousness — and class consciousness. He precisely lacks class consciousness at this point, because class consciousness is not only consciousness that you're a member of a class, it's consciousness of the class system as a set of structures determining how you see yourself. This is exactly what is obscured.

The moment he becomes aware of his class status, he ceases to be aware of class as a tower over him. The rest of the novel — to cut a really quite long story short — he comes into money — and I won't spoil the whole thing for you by telling you how he does that — he comes into money and — ach! I can't even really talk about it. (*Mark puts his face in his hands.*) It's one of the most horrible scenes in the whole of English literature. He comes into money and then, of course, he fully identifies with the ruling class — or tries to — but he's awkward. He doesn't really fit in with them. *(He sighs.)* Because he knows that he doesn't have the background. "Old money's better than new", as Roxy Music said. *(Laughter.)* And to give Bryan Ferry credit, he lived up to that![7] Anyway...

STUDENT #9: It's also self-knowledge of his social situation, I think, which is something that...

MF: Yeah, but his self-knowledge is precisely reified. It's a reified form of knowledge. It's ideology, which is to do with shame — intense shame. And when Joe — Joe the blacksmith who's looked after him, because he's an orphan — comes to London to visit him [when Pip is older and richer], Pip is ashamed *of him*! Pip is ashamed of him and he shows this shame to Joe, which is just unbearable at this point.

Not everyone will endure these traumas necessarily, when they try to move from one class to another, but it's not as simple as acquiring wealth or acquiring means of production, which is partly what is problematic about the Marxist definition of it anyway — the strict Marxist definition. Because, OK, if it's about ownership of the means of production *only*, then I could acquire the means of production tomorrow. In theory, that could happen to anybody — if you win the lottery. So, we need to account for what it is that *fixes* people in relation to their ownership (or not) of the means of production. Some people accept that they're never going to own anything, whereas others think the opposite. *Of course, I'm the owner. Of course, I'm not going to work. I'm not going to be a worker like* that. It's not that easy to move from one group to another. I think that's probably clearer from the Hartsock thing, that it's not that easy to move from being in the dominant group to being in the subordinate group, and vice versa.

What was the second question? I've forgotten now... Oh, yes, about the disappearance of the working class. Next week we sort of pause that story before the disappearance of the working class. It's when there was still a working class. But we can say that this is where we are now — where we *allegedly* are now. This is what we're endlessly told. Nothing could be more topical. Suddenly we're hearing about class again, but we've been told for years that class doesn't really exist. *No, we're all middle class now*. Nobody's saying that now. It's really interesting. Partly because they want to scapegoat the white working class! (*Laughs.*) We're hearing about class so that a certain ethnicised class can be blamed for things...

I think partly that reflects the complications of what has happened in capitalism when there *isn't* such a simple relationship between the ownership of the means of production and domination, in the way there used to be. But now that capital is so free-floating from production in the old sense — it's not about *I've got a factory making shoes* — that isn't the way things go, because of everything Marx said. When capital runs the show, shoes aren't only significant in terms of what they can be realised in terms of capital. Then you get capital itself and all this stuff... Of course, I can't understand it... But you're not supposed to understand it, any more than we were supposed to understand the Roman Catholic church in the time of the Middle Ages. *You're not supposed to understand it! Economy is theology!* Economics *is* the science of reification, you could say.

Part of what that means is there are different ways of looking at what's happened. So-called "post-Fordism", which we'll come onto — the shift away, certainly in the global north, from the manufacturing model, male workers, nine-to-five jobs for forty hours a week for forty years of your life — the shift away from that to flexibility, precariousness, the outsourcing of manufacturing to the third world, all that sort of thing... You could say that all of that was done in order to prevent class consciousness from developing. Because class consciousness *was* strong! It was strong. It was manifest. People understood themselves in those terms. They had made gains — significant gains. Capital wanted a way of overturning that. It came up with all of this stuff! And, at a point of high magic, made the very concept of class disappear! Which was *unthinkable*! It was *unthinkable* in Britain or the US! (And other countries... I don't know about other countries — well, I do a bit — but I can't speak confidently about those countries.) It's *unthinkable* in the Seventies that you could say that class would basically disappear as a basic form of self-understanding within twenty years. But it did. It did for a while. But did that *mean* that?

There're at least two levels of what class is, then, aren't there? There's class as a form of consciousness and there's class as a form of domination. The forms of domination persist but the forms of consciousness have been broken, you could say. And so, I think what you're describing is the trap that was set. It's almost as if they read this... Well, it's not "almost", they did do that. They know how class consciousness is produced. Because it's easier to produce it in conditions where there is physical proximity. When people can talk to each other together, then they can... When people have common experiences and can talk about them, then you've got the potential for developing consciousness very quickly. That's why workers aren't allowed to talk to one another! One place where I worked, when I worked in Further Education, the Head of Human Resources, who was exasperated by the development of some sort of class consciousness amongst their teachers, was like, "Well, you can't just sit in the pub and talk to each other!" *(Laughter.)* She actually said that! *What do you mean?!* It was like the usually unspoken rule — you're not supposed to do that. You can go to a pub and just talk rubbish, but you can't go to a pub and talk about the conditions of your work together. Don't do that. You can't do that. *(Laughs.)*

Look at it this way: What does capital want to get out of it? What must capital always do? Capital must always — if you go back to Marcuse — must prevent that awareness amongst people that they could live differently and have more control over their own lives. It *must* prevent that. It *has to* do it, and it has to *keep* doing it. Capitalists moan about hard work — and it is hard work! It never stops. It always has to keep preventing that potential.

It has to be prevented in universities as well. Universities were a red base — so-called. Marketisation: they're not making any money out of it — it's not about that! It's just about stopping the conditions for certain kinds of consciousness developing. Because people were taken out of the workplace for a while — young people — taken out of the workplace, free from those imperatives, and it's about time, right? In order to raise consciousness, you need time. And that's the difficulty, always.

Say you've done your day of work and then you go home. Are you going to leave the house now? *I'm tired!* Then you've done a double day of work — you've done a full day of work and then you've done domestic work on top of that, which is still overwhelmingly done by women more than men. So, you've done that, then do you want to go out and raise your consciousness? *Yeah, OK, but... I'm kind of tired... (Laughter.)* We can laugh about it, but we all do this. We've all got forms of this. It's like healthy eating or something. We know it's better for you, but why don't we do it? You might know things but you're not able to act on them. We can't be hard on ourselves about it. Time-poverty is real. And that's what they've done! That's why they want it — scarcity of time! As Marcuse said, we could all be working much less now, but that's the insanity of it — the full insanity of the capitalist system! They produce an artificial scarcity of time in order to produce a *real* scarcity of natural resources. That's effectively what's happening. It's the production of spurious commodities that nobody wants, like slippers with the faces of alligators or whatever... Imagine, you see those sorts of things and the amount of work that's gone into them; the amount of effort that's gone into transporting them from wherever to get to Lewisham where they're less than a pound and no one wants them...

[Capitalism] has to continually inhibit the capacity for consciousness, and it's done a very good job. You could say that time is fundamental to the means of production — of everything! It also seems to be, in the world today, like some sort of fairy-tale where there's some magical golden machine in a room over there that can make anything you want. It's just there, but you don't have the time to go there. You can have this machine that is the most wondrous thing imaginable but, if you don't have the time to use it, it might as well not be there. And that's where we are at. That's where we are in terms of what human capacities are at the moment, and what the capacities of the things produced by humans are — or let's put it that way, for the moment — and what the capacity of human agency to use those things is! This is very divergent.

Read CEOs when they talk about what they do. It's not like the old vision of exploitation, where the fat ogres with cigars and top hats sit with their feet on the skulls of workers. It's not really like that — if it ever was! They lead by example, the capitalist class. They're just this weird form of addict — a work addict. (*Mark puts on a pompous voice.*) *Yeah, yeah, I get up at 4:30am, check 200 emails before going to the gym for half an hour, see my kid for fifteen minutes, go to work, work there until about 8:00pm, grab a quick dinner, work some more, go to bed, repeat.* That's not even a caricature, really! That's more or less what they say!

So, it's a generalised kind of condition of time-poverty. And of course, consciousness cannot develop in those conditions. Because consciousness is not automatic. That's the thing. It's not immediate! Immediate is another name for automatic. It's always vulnerable, that's the thing. It's always vulnerable to falling back into reified categories coming from immediacy. That requires this time of endless reconfirmation.

The ideal thing is that they give us things well within our own time. Imagine if you could invent something like that — where you'd just endlessly distract yourself; at any point in the world and at any time in the world you can be reached by the imperatives of capitalism... Imagine an object like that! What would it look like?

STUDENT #10: A phone?

MF: Well, yes, exactly! (*Laughs.*) So now we can understand why they distribute phones practically for nothing now. We can imagine phones used in another way, perhaps, but surely this is their function in a contemporary world? To ensure that we're tethered... The thing is, it's a direct inversion, right? All of their language of relationality and communication and all of that... Look, it's not that fucking hard for me to talk to you! It's not that hard! But it is hard if I've got no time.

So, first of all, they make it seem as if it's hard. And you need *this*. (*Mark gestures to a phone.*) You need capital in order to communicate with people, you need a product of capital in order to relate to another person. Of course, what that means is that you're really not related — or not straightforwardly, if we can talk about anything straightforwardly anymore in this Lukács world... But it means that everything is being hived off or routed through capital. So, capital installs itself as this kind of parasite — this is kind of where we'll go with Negri and Autonomia.[8] This is essentially their argument: capital will install itself as a parasite on human relationships. And that's clearly where we are.

You couldn't dream of it! Well, you could, but... It is the level of domination at which capital can encroach on people's minds now. Even thirty or forty years ago, you wouldn't have dreamt of it. And that's partly the shift from this Fordist thing. *You're at work*. And, again, this is problematic, and interesting from a gendered point of view. This is the way capital operates with equality. It used to be the case that only women did the "double day", but now everyone does the "double day" in one form or another. You could say that, OK, men might not be doing housework still, but they're not sitting beyond the imperatives of capitalism in the evening. No, no! Just think about it: when male workers of the classic Fordist type went home — OK, so they were engaged in social reproduction which was for the benefit of capitalism as well as for their own benefit — but they weren't subjected to the direct imperatives of capital at home. There was a qualitative shift in life. Again, there are gendered problems of all sorts in this picture. It's not like it was a great time. But now there is no freedom from the imperatives of capital. And, as I say, it's a kind of voluntary compulsion, right? If that makes sense... I've just thought that [those two terms are contradictory]... But nobody makes you, in that sense. Nobody makes you own a phone. And if you do own it, nobody makes you go on social media. And, of course, if you're on social media, then you are producing for capitalism.

STUDENT #11: I think sometimes now, when you apply for jobs, they check through your social media, and they need to check these platforms. So, you kind of need one in some ways now.

MF: Yeah, so you need one. It's part of your responsibility for yourself that you have to curate your own subjectivity. But it's also that you're *producing* it. It's nothing without you. There's no social media, by definition, unless we're on it. Some argue, in the strict Marxist sense, whether this can be considered productive of capital but, meaning aside and the precise semantic details about it, it's clear that it depends on our participation in it. And that participation is, as it were, freely given — in a double sense: it's freely given in that nobody makes me and, secondly, nobody pays me.

But you also have to see what might be going on in that time. What used there to be for people to do? The working class might go to night school. They might go to a trade union night school. They might go to trade union reading groups, which a lot of people used to do where they read things like Lukács.

I think this is very complicated on lots of levels now.

There's a good piece by Gary Younge — I don't know if people read it — in *the Guardian* about Trump. He spent about a month hanging out in a typical town in the US and, he says, look, when you take away the union and the factory, you also take away the webs of connection that were around those things.[9] And the result of that is this kind of atomisation; of people falling back into their own private space. You notice that one of the big themes of the US election was drugs — the amount of young people who are on drugs. This became a key factor, and Trump's appeal was his appearing to care about this, and talk about it.

STUDENT #12: This subversion that you were talking about, I think, is exactly this subversion of immediacy and negation, as if, maybe at the time that Lukács was writing this, immediacy was the logic by which capitalism was dictating subjects to think about themselves in terms of their ability to gain consciousness, when mediation was actually the proper way to gain consciousness.

But now, something that was striking to me when I was reading this was that, now that everything is mediated, immediacy seems to be more of a radical practice.

MF: No, because... What do you mean by mediated though? I think you're conflating two senses of "mediated" — conflating this Hegelian-Marxist sense of "mediated" with a more ordinary sense of "mediated".

"Mediated" just means that it's not immediately given in experience. And it really has some relation to totality. That's, I think, what's at stake for Lukács here. It's not that people are now in a totality. Is it?

STUDENT #12: But they are?

MF: Well, they're *conscious* of being in the totality.

STUDENT #12: Well, I think having the consciousness is much harder. If the bourgeoisie, as the masters of the capitalist order, were incapable of understanding that system of interrelations, now masses of today's capitalists are very well aware of it. Because they use something like

Facebook, so they must be aware of it. So, there is still some sort of totality at work, but it is *deeply* mediated — as it was, maybe, two hundred years ago — but the ones who create it are aware of it. They know it, whereas the bourgeoisie [at the time Lukács was writing] was incapable of being conscious of that interrelationship... No?

MF: Well, I mean, why does Mark Zuckerberg create Facebook?

STUDENT #12: Sorry?

MF: Why does Mark Zuckerberg create Facebook? Why does he do it?

STUDENT #12: Maybe at the time he didn't know, but it took him a while to understand...

MF: Well, he doesn't know, but something might know. That's the thing. Capital can know, right? Capital can know, because capital is like evolution: it selects for things. Capital has agency. Mark Zuckerberg has a kind of idiotic compulsion to like, *errghh I wanna make loads of money and, like, impress some girls.* (*Laughter.*) As we see in [David Fincher's 2010 film] *The Social Network*, which is a brilliant film, I think. Really... It's almost unprecedented, *The Social Network*, don't you think? And also the meticulousness of the construction of its historical moment, in terms of the forms of technology it's working with. We'll come to that later. We'll come to that later.

So, he has those motives but that doesn't mean that capital doesn't have its own ends and designs inside, without there being any conscious agent that's sitting behind it all. Otherwise it's just a conspiracy, isn't it? The thing is, it's a systemic tendency. It's a systemic tendency. Now, of course, at a certain point, there are humans who make self-conscious decisions at crucial points, but there are also people like Zuckerberg who are puppets of capital without any kind of reflection.

STUDENT #12: The reason I was asking is because of this notion of immediacy and negation and dialectic being... Because I guess I just don't fully understand it? I don't know *how* to understand it...

MF: (*Laughs.*) Yeah...

STUDENT #12: Because, in a way, immediacy has to be... We have to sidestep immediacy and just pass behind it and reach consciousness through some kind of mediation...? We were talking about the possibilities for social mobility and how hard that actually is, and that people get stuck, to some degree, to the immediate environment which they live in, which means that immediacy, to an extent, can't be stepped behind...

MF: Right, OK. Well, I think we should have a look at some actual quotations.
(*Mark starts looking through the text.*)
OK, this is good: what is immediacy — "an illusion which is itself the product of the habits of thought and feeling of mere immediacy where the immediately given form of the objects, the fact of their existing here and now and in this particular way appears to be primary, real and objective, whereas their 'relations' seem to be secondary and subjective".[10]
"Unable to discover further mediations, unable to comprehend the reality and the origin of bourgeois society as the product of the same subject that has

'created' the comprehended totality of knowledge, *its ultimate point of view, decisive for the whole of its thought, will be that of immediacy*".[11]

"The observer stands outside the landscape, for were this not the case it would not be possible for nature to become a landscape at all".[12]

In order to see things as outside you, you can't be in them.

"The historical knowledge of the proletariat begins with knowledge of the present, with the self-knowledge of its own social situation and with the elucidation of its necessity..."[13]

Yeah. "Mediation would not be possible were it not for the fact that the empirical existence of objects is itself mediated and only appears to be unmediated in so far as the awareness of mediation is lacking so that the objects are torn from the complex of their true determinants and placed in artificial isolation".[14]

"...if the bourgeoisie is held fast in the mire of immediacy from which the proletariat is able to extricate itself, this is neither purely accidental nor a purely theoretical scientific problem".[15]

Let's just read a bit more. It's quite nice to go back to it, actually, when you've had the discussion, because it immediately feels less opaque, the writing, I think. It might not be leaping off the page, but I think it does seem more tractable and lucid after a bit of discussion. *(Laughs.)*

"For the proletariat, social reality... appears in the first instance as the pure object of societal events. In every aspect of daily life in which the individual worker imagines himself to be the subject of his own life he finds this to be an illusion that is destroyed by the immediacy of his existence".[16]

"...because of the split between subjectivity and

objectivity induced in man by the compulsion to objectify himself as a commodity, the situation becomes one that can be made conscious".[17]

"Above all the worker can only become conscious of his existence in society when he becomes aware of himself as a commodity".[18] That's part of this dialectical process. He has to first of all accept the objectification of himself, or the objectification of herself. "As we have seen, his immediate existence integrates him as a pure, naked object into the production process. Once this immediacy turns out to be the consequence of a multiplicity of mediations, once it becomes evident how much it presupposes, then the fetishistic forms of the commodity system begin to dissolve: in the commodity the worker recognises himself and his own relations with capital. Inasmuch as he is incapable in practice of raising himself above the role of object his consciousness is *the self-consciousness of the commodity*; or in other words it is the self-knowledge, the self-revelation of the capitalist society founded upon the production and exchange of commodities."[19]

When fetishism dissolves... What is fetishism? That's a big question, but in a Marxist sense it is, then, this magicking away of the totality, or the magicking away of the *actual material conditions* which produce something.

STUDENT #12: Fetishisation seems to be quite contrary to reification, in a way. Because reification tries to make everything that could be abstract real. Fetishisation tries to conceal the actual concreteness of how things take place in mystification...

MF: Right. Good. Yeah. But obviously they work together. They're complementary processes.

So, "when the worker knows himself as a commodity

his knowledge is practical. *That is to say, this knowledge brings about an objective structural change in the object of knowledge*".[20] That's what I was trying to say earlier, about how this immediately changes. Perhaps "immediate" isn't the right word, given... (*Trails off to laughter*) "In this consciousness and through it the special objective character of labour as a commodity, its 'use-value' (i.e. its ability to yield surplus produce) which like every use-value is submerged without a trace in the quantitative exchange categories of capitalism, now awakens and becomes *social reality*. The special nature of labour as a commodity which in the absence of this consciousness acts as an unacknowledged driving wheel in the economic process now objectifies itself by means of this consciousness".[21]

"...the fact that this commodity is able to become aware of its existence as a commodity does not suffice to eliminate the problem. For the unmediated consciousness of the commodity is, in conformity with the simple form in which it manifests itself, precisely an awareness of abstract isolation and of the merely abstract relationship — external to consciousness — to those factors that create it socially".[22] So it's not enough just to think, *I am a commodity*. More has to be done than that.

"Thus, the knowledge that social facts are not objects but relations between men" — sic., of course, because it's heavily gendered — "is intensified to the point where facts are wholly dissolved into processes".[23]

"This image of a frozen reality that nevertheless is caught up in an unremitting, ghostly movement at once becomes meaningful when this reality is dissolved into the process of which man is the driving force. This can be seen only from the standpoint of the proletariat because the meaning of these tendencies is the abolition of capitalism and so for the bourgeoisie to become conscious of them would be tantamount to suicide".[24] That's partly why bourgeois class consciousness can never really fully exist.

The bourgeoisie can have consciousness and have common interests as a class — clearly, they do — but they can't have consciousness of the class system, you could say. Only the proletariat can have common interests, shared consciousness, *and* consciousness of the class system. The bourgeoisie are *products* of the class system, right? By their nature, that's what they are. They're the products and the reproducers of the class system; the proletariat is the destroyer of the class system. The bourgeoisie only exists in the class system; the proletariat exists both inside it and outside it. It has to be that way, because it has to be inside it — *because it is*; that's the way we are under capitalism — but it also has to be partly outside, otherwise there'd be no possibility of movement to the outside.

"But as soon as mankind has clearly understood and hence *restructured* the foundations of its existence truth acquires a wholly novel aspect. When theory and practice are united it becomes possible to change reality and when this happens the absolute and its 'relativistic' counterpart will have played their historical role for the last time. For as the result of these changes we shall see the disappearance of that reality which the absolute and the relative expressed in like manner".[25]

There is no absolute because everything dissolves into a process *at this point*. And I think this is what he's suggesting, right? Just massive de-reification, and the opening up of the possibility to change reality at every level. "This process *begins* when the proletariat becomes conscious of its own class point of view".[26]

"The individual can never become the measure of all things. For when the individual confronts objective reality he is faced by a complex of ready-made and unalterable objects which allow him only the subjective responses of recognition or rejection. Only the class can relate to the whole of reality in a practical revolutionary way".[27] And, as I say, with Nancy Hartsock, you can see that this concept of class can be replaced by other forms of subordination.

"Reification is, then, the necessary, immediate reality of every person living in capitalist society. It can be overcome only by *constant and constantly renewed efforts to disrupt the reified structure of existence by concretely relating to the concretely manifested contradictions of the total development, by becoming conscious of the immanent meanings of these contradictions for the total development*".[28] This is totality versus immediacy again. "This reality is not, it becomes".[29] *There is no fixed form of reality*, because that itself is a reification. Reality is only a process of becoming.

"For a possibility to be realised, for a tendency to become actual, what is required is that the objective components of a society should be transformed; their functions must be changed and with them the structure and content of every individual object. But it must never be forgotten: *only the practical class consciousness of the proletariat* possesses this ability to transform things. Every contemplative, purely cognitive stance leads ultimately to a divided relationship to its object".[30] "Even the proletariat can only overcome reification as long as it is oriented towards practice".[31] So there's the emphasis on practice.

So yeah, "*the practical class consciousness*": he's trying to unite these two things, which, perhaps in bourgeois terms, would be opposite — which would be consciousness and practice. Class consciousness is always practical in that way, anyway. That's the difference from the ordinary sense in which we know consciousness. Consciousness *is there*. It doesn't require a practice to sustain it. The brain will do it for you, regardless, on some level.

It's not that I think, having read those out quickly, we can go home happy. But I think it is worth reading out loud, especially when you've only got it on a screen, the brain just tends to skip ahead.

It's not obscurantist. It's just heavily stylised, because of the inheritance of Hegel and this question of immediacy.

I think we can take this forward, then, as the key problem. What we've talked about today, the question of consciousness. This is the question I'll be posing for the rest of the module. How does consciousness get raised and how does it get depressed? Next week we'll look at ways in which it can be — and was — raised.

The last gasp: this is from the book *Stayin' Alive: The Last Days of the Working Class*. But it wasn't just a kind of failure. It was dramatic. What happened in the early Seventies in the US and in Italy and other countries, going on until late into the Seventies, was the development of a new kind of democratic socialism, a libertarian communism that broke from the old authoritarian structures of Cold War labour. It was also about making existential demands about the quality of work. A lot of trade unions had accepted that they were basically arguing about wages, not so much about what work would actually be like, what life would actually be like. The ultimate aim would be getting rid of work anyway.

But in the early Seventies in the US, as we'll see next week, there is this explosion of this new consciousness, which was almost a kind of intersectionality at this time: the Women's Movement becoming articulated with workers, articulated with civil rights and post-civil rights struggles. It was an explosive combination of alliances of the broad Left, and this kind of open equality...

I'm not really sure how we're going to approach this text next week. It's very different to this. It's a historical narrative text. It's not a theoretical text. But the theoretical text is easier to teach, in a way, because you can do concepts. But this is a story, so I'm not sure how we'll deal with it...

(Recording ends abruptly.)

Lecture Four:
"Union Power and Soul Power"

28 November 2016

MARK FISHER: How do you teach history? Theory, even though it's hard, has principles behind it that can be explained. It's just there, isn't it. *(Laughs.)*

Alright. So, what are the new developments we can see in this text? Obviously, I've included it as a practical example of some of the things we talked about last week.

Last week we were theorising, initially, class consciousness via Lukács, and then a kind of feminist consciousness. But more broadly, now, we're looking at the question of group consciousness. How does group consciousness develop?

What I wanted from this text, really, was to look at an example of where that consciousness *practically* developed in a historical moment. What were people's responses to it?

(Silence.)

Let's put it this way: did this surprise you? Let's look at it in relation to today, now, as well. What is the promise on offer that starts to emerge in these struggles at this time? And how does that compare to the situation that we're in today, do you think?

STUDENT #1: I think it's interesting, what he does first. First, he talks about one event happening in 1969 and then comes back to one that developed in 1935. It links what happened in the Thirties with what happened in the Seventies. But it's very different. In the Thirties, there was maybe a good solution for the working class, but in the Seventies it's like these efforts or these attempts to drive the working class to a struggle is a failure. What's happening nowadays is not a working class like we know or what we are reading in the Seventies, so I'm not sure how to trace the link between the Seventies or today... Maybe today there is another type of class...

MF: OK. That's a really important thing to pick up on: this parallel with the Thirties.

The Thirties was *the* previous great period of labour power — "labour" not in the English context of the Labour Party but labour as in organised labour. This is when organised labour really asserted itself, when there was a strong communist presence within the US — the Communist Party was pretty strong, etc. So, there was a strong Left. In Cowie's narrative, the Seventies becomes a kind of replay of the Thirties. But it's not a perfect replay. That's not the way that history works.

What is it that makes the end of the Sixties and the Seventies *like* the Thirties, then? What happened in between? What happened in between the Thirties and the Seventies?

STUDENT #2: I think what is interesting in this text is the shift of leadership within the struggle of the union. That seems to be defining the fact that the struggle was not as powerful anymore, in the Seventies.

MF: Yes. I think that is partly an answer to the question posed. So, what was the leadership like, then, in between the Thirties and the Seventies?

The Thirties was a period of great militancy. It wasn't

only about trade union power. There was quite a lot of trade union power between the Thirties and the Seventies. But what was the difference in the way that power operated in, say, the Forties, Fifties, and the early Sixties? That's what's behind your question, really.

STUDENT #1: More adherence to power? Some [trade union] leaderships, or some leaders, are supporting some kind of democratic party more closely? Maybe? I don't know…

MF: I think it's partly the integration of unions into American society — the biggest one was the CIO[1] — which was the biggest symbol of organised labour in the US, but it was Cold War unionism, really. It was defined by anti-communism, in part. It was defined by its connection to, and by its being fitted into, the establishment. I think he says at one point, in 1972… The 1972 election, which is something that we'll come back to later when we look at Nixon, was this pivotal moment where there was a split between the counterculture, on the one hand, and Nixon on the other. That's basically what happened.

George McGovern was the Democrat candidate for the election in '72. He was not supported by the big established unions. In fact, they said they would neither support him nor Nixon. And given how right-wing Nixon was, that was a bit like the trade unions saying they were not going to support — well, I don't know if the analogy really works — it's like they were saying they were not going to support Hillary Clinton or Trump, which seems legitimate to me in lots of ways [in our contemporary moment]. But in '72, saying you didn't support either candidate is, in effect, an endorsement for the Republican candidate, right? Given that you would expect trade unions to support the left-wing party, which was the Democrats. But the refusal to endorse McGovern effectively meant that they were supporting Nixon.

Why was that the case? Because, from their point of view, McGovern's campaign was supported by a load of crazies. It was a coalition of Civil Rights, counterculture — the whole constellation of the counterculture, really. But without much representation from the traditional basis of the working class, you could say.

So, I think what we had in '72 was something that's really persisted until today. What you also have to say is that this is the most ringing defeat for a candidate in the history of American elections. McGovern was *absolutely hammered* by Nixon in '72. Of course, there was a further twist to this tale in that it was a kind of poison chalice for Nixon to win that presidency, because what happened in that term — in Nixon's next term in office — was the most famous scandal in political history. So, he wins power, but he faces Watergate really quickly [afterwards].[2]

So, there we are. That was part of the story here, which points to a way in which the Seventies was not just a repetition of the Thirties. In a way, both the Thirties and the Seventies failed. There was not a working-class revolution in either the Thirties or the Seventies, so they both failed. But we still haven't answered the question... What was new about the Seventies, then, that wasn't there in the Thirties? It wasn't just that the Seventies was this failed version of the Thirties...

STUDENT #3: The Vietnam War? Attitudes towards race?

MF: Right, OK. The Vietnam War was a big deal. The Vietnam War and the counterculture were kind of mirrors of one another, right?

STUDENT #4: Increases in automation and globalisation? So that labour had less power in the Seventies?

MF: Yes. That's by the end, isn't it, that he starts to stress those things. Why it failed, in a way, was the increase in automation. But let's take those two things separately.

The Vietnam War, first of all, was the mirror of the counterculture in many ways. And the two were interlocked. The counterculture was organised around opposition to the Vietnam War and we'll come to that...

STUDENT #3: And the anti-authoritarianism that came with it.

MF: Yeah, and we'll come to that in a few weeks when we come to the Penny Lewis text when we look at the ways in which the Nixon strategy served to initiate this idea of a kind of reactionary working class — or not initiate but *work with* this kind of trope of a reactionary working class — which was partly there in the dynamics of the 1972 election, where you had a counterculture, not only versus the establishment, but also the counterculture versus the established working class and the leaders of the established working class who, as I said, effectively aligned themselves with Nixon against these new anti-authoritarian countercultural currents.

That was part of what was new about it, right? What we're seeing described here, partly, in this chapter, is the kind of fusion of the counterculture with unionism. But by '72, we're already seeing that start to fail. So, there's two things going on here at least. One of which is this new and unprecedented form of anti-authoritarian leftism, that also draws upon key struggles — it isn't just about class, it's also about race and it's also about gender in particular. That's what he stresses. This is new. This is relatively new. But it's important to stress that, often, we can talk about the Left and its embedded sexism and racism — and no doubt that is always true — although it's certainly less true of the Left than other areas of society — it's not as if areas of culture dominated by the Right were less racist and less sexist than on the Left — but it's more likely there are pockets of the progressive in the Left, even back in the Thirties — that's the caveat. However, by the Seventies, then, in some of the struggles that he's highlighting here, there was this growing recognition of the insufficiency of — or the problems with — assuming the white male worker's outlook as the norm.

And this is exciting, right? That's what I like about this. There's a series of struggles — they are exciting. They bring together diverse groups of people. They coalesce around so-called minority groups. But what does he also stress? What is the difference in the nature of these struggles to previous struggles?

STUDENT #3: Young people?

MF: Young people are key. But what does young also connote? What does it connect with?

STUDENT #4: Hedonism?

MF: Yeah, OK, but more broadly? The question of hedonism — of pleasure, enjoyment, etc. — how does that translate into a set of demands in relation to struggle?

STUDENT #3: They don't want to be on a factory line. They want more power and more challenges in their work.

MF: OK, so there are qualitative demands about the nature of work, existential demands about the nature of work, in addition to quantitative demands about pay and working hours, etc. And this is partly the shift that we'll look at from Fordism into post-Fordism.

Fordism essentially accepts a more-or-less nine-to-five picture of work. It even assumes the white male worker. So, the demands are based around remuneration for that work. In effect, you exchange boredom for security, under the Fordist model. On this model, that's not enough. It demands for [the] quality of work — what is it actually like at work? — to shift. And that is partly a pressure from the hedonistic dominations of the counterculture.

STUDENT #1: And something you said: the perception of communism as a threat. In the Thirties, it wasn't. Now it's seen as a threat, in the Seventies. It is the enemy.

MF: Yeah, the Seventies was clearly during the Cold War. The Soviets become the *official* enemy, as it were, after the Second World War, and many of the key trade unions lined up in support of the idea that the key problem was communism. In the Thirties, I think it was much more inchoate: there wasn't any one enemy, there wasn't any one problem.

And, of course, what was the key historical event of the Thirties?

STUDENT #3: The Great Depression.

MF: Yeah, exactly. The Great Depression lent strength to the far left.

But in the late Sixties and early Seventies, we're not in a situation to break, right? The situation is quite different. In fact, as he suggests at the end of the chapter, it was the recession, starting in '73, that put an end to these kinds of struggles.

Why was that?

STUDENT #4: The beginnings of neoliberalism?...

MF: Yeah, but I think neoliberalism, as a set of policies and ideas, pre-existed this. It goes back to at least the Forties, I think.

STUDENT #4: But it went mainstream...

MF: Yeah, exactly, but I think, in this moment — why it's interesting and why I want to stress it — it cleared the ground for neoliberalism to come in at the end of the Seventies. That's part of what we can look at when we read Naomi Klein. When we come onto Chile as the example, it's pretty clear that — with the US, you can say, it was a much more organic failure... I don't really like the word "organic" for lots of reasons... But there were multiple reasons why these kinds of struggles did not produce a new hegemonic leftist force in the early Seventies. But, with Chile, it was much more simple. There was a neoliberal coup, ultimately, and straightforwardly. The CIA backed the coup against the Allende government, knocked down the Allende government, and turned Chile into this kind of laboratory in which the neoliberal policies could be tested out for the first time.

I guess, following this, there's a kind of narrative... There's a bittersweet quality to this narrative, isn't there? That's one of the things that I would want to take from it. There was an unprecedented ferment, excitement, fervour, newly anti-authoritarian, diverse leftism at the same time as there was this dying curve, this movement, this drift in towards neoliberal domination — what I would call capitalist realism — both at the same time, really, going on. That's why this book is called *The Last Days of the Working Class*.

But there was a glorious quality to some of these struggles. It's worse, in lots of ways, than that things just went into a gradual decline. *There was a strong working class, it gradually declined in the early Seventies, and then neoliberalism took over.* This isn't the story here, right? At least, I don't take this to be the story. The story is: there was a strong working class, elements of which had been co-opted, but there was a new vision of class politics that was emerging at the time, which could renew and reinvigorate class struggle in an unprecedented way, but that ended very quickly, almost as soon as it had started.

I think last week we [briefly] talked about the dynamics of work in Sartre's text, *The Critique of Dialectical Reason*, which, as I said, I haven't read — few have, because of the size of it and the fact it was written as kind of speed ravings — but that's one of the dynamics that he talks about: this shift between the kind of vital heat of insurgency, when things are new and there's a struggle against something, and the moment of consolidation, when the former revolutionary or rebellious forces become integrated into a kind of new establishment. Clearly, that was one of the dynamics at work here with the trade unions. At the top end they become co-opted; they become, in many cases — as we see with this initial story about the Yablonski killings[3] — highly corrupt and integrated into American society in the worst way.

But then, here we have it, this vision of renewal, this possibility of renewal.

Perhaps we can reflect back and make the connections with last week, in terms of the question of class consciousness or group consciousness. How has that developed through these struggles, do you think?

(Silence.) What are the problems?

STUDENT #4: Does it suggest the failure of group consciousness...? Neoliberalism allowed us to think of ourselves as more individual so group consciousness no longer worked.

MF: Yeah, I think this is one of the things going on in this text. I'm using the term "group consciousness" to incorporate class consciousness and other forms of consciousness... But is that the right way to look at it? Is class consciousness different in kind from feminist consciousness or consciousness of race, do you think?

Let's look at it this way: one of the things that they tried to do — and succeeded [in doing] — was the divide and rule tactic. That's one of the things that he emphasises, isn't it? Turning, particularly, whites against blacks, in order to stoke up resentment between the two. And one of the things he picks up on and one of the things I wanted to look at in this module is the development of resentment as the driving force of reaction in the period since the Seventies. Because resentment, in a way, is a form of anti-solidarity, is a form of anti-consciousness.[4] Because resentment is, to me, *I'm not getting something that somebody else should get*, not that *we should all get more*, which you could say is the basis of class consciousness.

One of the things I would like to look at, from this in relation to today, then, is that what we're seeing in the Seventies is the decentring of class. What is initially a decentring of class... What we're seeing *now* is the return of class!

STUDENT #1: Now?

MF: Yes! In between, first of all, what we had was decentring and then there was, for all intents and purposes, the removal of class. By the Nineties, let's say, class has effectively been removed as a category from political discourse. I want to look at this later, the question of the middle — the importance of the middle, the growth of the middle — this idea from John Prescott and the New Labour politicians at the time that "we're all middle class now". This is one of the things I mentioned in the first week. That is an *impossible* typology. *It is impossible*. Not everyone can be middle class. Not everyone can be in the middle. What are we in the middle of?

I think what's interesting about that phrase is the doubleness of it. It's both disavowing class at the same time as its assuring the impossibility of completely overcoming it. Because if we're all middle class then, really, there is no such thing as a class struggle anymore. But hold on! We're still talking about class, though? So, we still have to use the term class but in the very attempt to eliminate the concept.

So I think, in Britain and the US — the two societies that I have a reasonable knowledge of — you can lay it in from elsewhere — particularly in Britain in the Seventies, the idea that class would be substantially removed from people's self-understanding would have been remarkable. But by the Nineties, it can seem to be the case that class no longer exists.

But I think with the big developments this year, what we've seen is the return of class. But class without class consciousness — or that's what I would argue. In the UK, with Brexit, and in the US with the Trump victory, both of those substantially depended on class and class dynamics, but not on the assertion of a self-conscious proletarian agency — on the contrary, almost the opposite.

This is partly why this text is important, then. Why

this is worth holding onto is because of the possibility of an intersectional class politics.

I think when the term "intersectional" is used now, it's often used to mean something which excludes class politics altogether, and you'll see a lot of arguments like this around the current US election, whether it was Trump being able to play the class card — ludicrously, in lots of ways.[5] How could a millionaire, or he's a billionaire, isn't he? Anyway, he's a property developer, someone who inherited his money — it's not like he was a self-made man... How could a billionaire property developer somehow plausibly ventriloquise the concerns, anxieties, the subjectivity of members of the working class? That's a good one, but he *did* manage to do it. There're complex reasons for that. Partly there was a phantasmatic one... Part of the way in which the suppression of class consciousness operates is via the fantasy recruitment of the subordinated into identification with a career... There was a piece in the *Harvard Business Review*, actually, making this distinction between the "rich" and the "professionals", which argued essentially — this goes back to the question of resentment — that many members of the working class will resent professionals — lawyers, doctors, lecturers, etc. — but they will identify with the rich.[6] They have no problems with the rich. I think that's partly because people are encouraged to think they're already rich, they just haven't got money yet — a bit like Lady Gaga, when she said, "I was already famous, it's just people didn't know yet". *(Laughter.)* That's the way everything works. That's why, often, poorer members of society will oppose tax cuts against the rich. Why? Because they're already rich themselves, in their minds. It's not like this is a failure on their part, or a delusion. They're encouraged into this identification.

(Silence.)

Sorry, that was a whole big parenthesis and now I've lost where I was.

OK, so I guess what we're seeing now is the end of — the coming-up out of — an inversion of what we see here. In the Seventies, with the trade unions, class was the great tractor narrative [that pulled all other concerns along with it] and then it was being decentred. And although it's this moment of decentring, it was still there! But this wasn't to the exclusion of other kinds of struggle, in particular race and gender. All three could be articulated together, at least to some extent. And so there was a way in which you could say class — if you pardon the term — trumped, for instance, race — it was not because class was more important than race, but as we can see now, race is used as a way of deflecting and deflating class consciousness.

So, class consciousness, as we emphasised last week, is not, then, just a recognition of an already existing state of affairs. If I'm conscious of this table, I'm simply conscious of something that is already there. But if I become, as we saw with Lukács, part of a conscious collective agency, then something has actually shifted because of that consciousness already. The nature of the social world has already shifted by virtue of the development of that consciousness.

So, class, you could say, is not really *there*. It is there to be produced as this form of solidarity, which could bring together black workers and white workers, for instance. So it goes against the actual dominant tendencies of the social world, which were precisely meant to suppress the possibilities of those forms of consciousness by keeping those workers competing with one another, and resenting that fact.

OK, so those are the kind of glimmers, then — well, it's more than a glimmer — these struggles took place over a number of years, they echoed what was going on in Europe and other areas of the world... So, there was a powerful sense, then, of a shift. I guess part of my story is that what happened was this decentring went too far. Class becomes removed. We then have race, gender, other kinds of struggle, coming to the fore, but all of them are fatally distorted once class is taken out of the picture. Which isn't necessarily to say that class is more important than those other forms of identification or forms of struggle, it's just that when class is no longer there, it's like this void, this hole, which means that the given picture is necessarily incomplete. It's like I said, it's not like class ever really goes away. It's class consciousness that disappears, that subsides. Class itself doesn't go away. And actually, the re-emergence of class today has suited the Right and not the Left, because of the way it operates. Class becomes seen as a form of identitarian resentment, let's put it that way. This is something that the Right worked on developing since the end of the Sixties and this, again, is why Nixon is a key figure here.

Trump essentially repeats the same gestures that Nixon would before [him], which is to appeal to an identitarian working class. What do I mean by an identitarian working class? I mean a class that is defined not by its consciousness or by its agency but by particular identity characteristics that are prescribed to it.

STUDENT #4: It's sort of like the processes of reification then, in that sense?

MF: Yes, go on...

STUDENT #4: I guess, since the Seventies, there have been attempts to de-reify the class structure, an attempt to recode it as this not-concrete thing that doesn't exist, and then it proves how fickle that task, in the sense that, within the matter of a year, or a year or a half, it's just been re-reified and just made concrete again by certain right-wing parties.

MF: Yeah, but I don't think it's just in the last year or...

STUDENT #4: No, I was just wondering if that's what that process is.

MF: Oh, yeah, I think that's a good way of looking at it. Yeah. Exactly. I guess what I mean by "identitarian" is, partly then, a reified vision of what class is.

So, the rise of the Right, since the Seventies, the neoliberal Right, is partly to do with this petit bourgeois identification. You can retain your identity but you can become wealthier and you can become self-employed, so you don't have to lose the features of your subjectivity, or your existential life which you identify as being the definition of you, you can retain those, and they are what is understood as the class elements. Essentially, your cultural qualities — the way you speak, comportment, certain kinds of values, etc. — of your existing working class. These can remain the same, and you can get a lot richer.

But that form of identitarian capture of class is exactly what was necessary to neutralise class consciousness. That's the opposite of class consciousness, in that way. Class consciousness would not be about saying, "I have this set of properties now and this is what makes us share a class position". It's more like, "we have a class position in common in spite of whatever cultural, personal, subjective qualities we possess". And that once we act in accordance, once we think of ourselves as sharing this class consciousness, then we are transformed. Our transformation occurs.

It is partly, then, this question — from last week from Lukács — which is the class that can imagine or be the agent of the abolition of capitalism? It is the proletariat. Not because the proletariat possesses all the existing predicates, but because it occupies a position within the class struggle, and because it is defined by a set of common interests, which are interests defined against those of capital.

STUDENT #5: Didn't the Trump election create, more-or-less, a failed or different class consciousness, where there's not the proletariat and the bourgeoisie, but the common people and the politicians…

MF: Yes.

STUDENT #5: …because eventually Trump got all the votes from different kinds of people. He wanted the women's vote and he got a lot of the Hispanic vote as well, despite the fact he'd said terrible things about them, because he still created this consciousness of, well, he's not a politician so he's on our side. Despite my race, my gender, whatever it is, we are oppressed by a political class.

MF: Yes.

STUDENT #5: It's not true, maybe, but isn't that still a kind of consciousness that he raises? This is, more or less, like a teleological story of the forgotten people in the labour struggle. OK, we have the union, but the blacks are excluded or the Hispanics are excluded or the women are excluded, and then we just have a working class… Now

I've lost my thought... But the question I have, basically, is: could there be a bad aspect about class consciousness if there is a different kind of class? Because I guess you could create a consciousness of every kind of class, or of every kind of group? Because being self-conscious — as we talked about last week — about the feminist standpoint is realising that, OK, I'm not the enemy but the patriarchy is. But couldn't you create this for any kind of thing? It's not my fault that my clothes shrink, but it's the washing machine, and you could create a consciousness about this, but it's me using the washing machine wrong? (*Laughter and murmurs of disagreement.*) That's an exaggeration of this idea of consciousness. I could create this for any kind of thing, maybe, if I wanted to, and that's probably what happened with Trump...

STUDENT #1: But is that even Trump? Because in [Greece with] Syriza it happened the other way. Syriza was the image of the common class or the common people against these policies that destroyed a country, in the same way as Podemos in Spain. And they didn't win. So, it's not just a thing that happened with Trump. I think it's a question that arises from the 2008 [financial] crisis. Those who had the knowledge of the economy, they didn't work [together] to manage the economy. So it's the common people versus those who have the knowledge of the economy.

STUDENT #4: Yeah, that's precisely what I mean. What if we call it "postcapitalist desire", the enemy would be capitalism, but the consciousness is not: OK, it's capitalism [which] is the problem, but that it's the politicians in power...

STUDENT #1: But Trump is racist, he's misogynist, and

he's very rich... To an older person like that, that's the establishment, in a way.

STUDENT #4: But he's not a politician...

STUDENT #1: Yeah, but that's the only characteristic that is aside from the establishment. He's not a professional politician.

MF: I think there's at least two things at play in what you're asking, one of which is: how many different forms of consciousness can we have? Secondly, you implied there was a false consciousness. The washing machine thing is a false consciousness. It's simply wrong.

STUDENT #4: But I could still believe it.

MF: You could still believe it, yeah, but I think for Hartsock, consciousness necessarily is to do with truth, actually. Remember: she isn't a postmodern relativist. This is important. I think this is why it's powerful, this notion of a standpoint. It still holds on to the idea of truth. There are, in this picture, two standpoints — the dominant and the subordinated, you could say — starting off from class, from Marx — there's the proletariat and the bourgeoisie. There are these two standpoints, but one is false! One gives a true picture. You get a true picture *by virtue of being subordinated*. That's the thing, right? The subordinated have the truer picture because they have both pictures, in a way. The dominant are inside their own story.

STUDENT #1: But in which sense is consciousness about truth? Because now it seems that it's more about the word of the year: "post-truth".[7] In which sense is truth related with consciousness? Now — I'm talking about now.

MF: Yeah, I want to take this question up, seriously. Is this true, that there are standpoints that are more valid? That offer a truer perspective on society's social relations in this century? Is this true? Or is the postmodern version of relativism right that there is no truth? Is old-style Enlightenment objectivism right that there is a form of truth that has nothing to do with standpoints whatsoever but is instead independent from standpoints?

That's one set of questions, I think, about the relationship between truth and consciousness, but there is another set of questions that are about the practical politics that are about proliferating different forms of consciousness.

Is there a way of thinking about consciousness as different from identity, which is what I was trying to talk about earlier? Because, I guess, simply, identity would be a formula for how we are now and how we have been. Whereas consciousness, in its transformative dimension, would be about the transformed agent that appears when consciousness develops. It's not about how things are now, it's about what we might say are — this something we might come onto again later — the hyperstitional effects of when this identification occurs. What happens then?

I guess the issue is, then, what are the crucial antagonisms that define what society is and how it can be transformed — so the class, gender, race antagonisms, etc. — but there's no reason to stop there necessarily, is there? We could just carry on. But is that proliferation, in itself, even a political strategic problem? Or isn't there a way of saying, we can add all these things together, but the question is articulation.

STUDENT #5: Sorry, could you repeat that?

MF: Yeah, the question is articulation — of the linkage of different struggles.

STUDENT #5: Within the dominant narrative that's given by the dominant position, you mean?

MF: Well, against the dominant position, I think. So, you could say there is no practical problem, necessarily, with proliferating this stuff if there is linkage, if there is articulation. There is a problem if they are seen as contradicting one another, undermining one another. That's why, I guess, we could use the overall term "group consciousness" — a transformative group consciousness aimed at a radical shift out of where we are now.

STUDENT #6: I think it does become a political problem once these different kinds of struggles end up reinforcing an idea of individualism and — not necessarily consciousness — it's in the Cowie text, and he lists it as one of the reasons for the disillusion of the union struggles in the Seventies... "issues on both the Right and the Left" — and he lists a long list — "ERA, bussing, abortion, and affirmative action, as well as the general trend of what would later be labelled as 'identity politics' or 'rights consciousness'"[8] — so that this mix of issues, in place of group consciousness, affirmed individual consciousness, and that was one of the key reasons for the disillusion of the union struggle.

So yeah, it is a political issue, because it does move away from a group consciousness and towards more individual ideas.

MF: Well, it doesn't necessarily, because if you've got

gender, race, they're not individual, are they? They're kind of structural. Individual consciousness, almost by definition, couldn't be consciousness in the same way, right? It would be a different sense of consciousness. It would be an everyday sense of consciousness, which would be precisely an anti-consciousness in the Lukácsian sense. Because consciousness, in a sense of class consciousness, must be a sense of the way there are no individuals, really — there are only structural forces.

But, of course, I take your point. One of the things that did happen after this period was the development of this kind of anti-consciousness, you could say, with people seeing themselves as individuals and as not belonging to a class.

But I wonder if identity logic — taking identity as the model rather than class — is the issue here, for understanding those other forms of struggle. And this was the way in which the Right could capture these struggles. Because you could say it's not the positive features of actually existing women that define women as a revolutionary class. It's not the positive features of actually existing minority race groups that define them as a revolutionary class. It's their structural and antagonistic position and the potential for transformation that occurs once consciousness develops that makes them potentially revolutionary agents.

But if we're invited to understand ourselves by the features which we are held to already possess, this is a form of reification. X equals X. You are what you already identify with. I guess what I'm saying here is that, one of the things that played out in relation to the recent election in the US, was this old trope of class politics versus identity politics, but what I'm saying is that the reason that that occurs is because of the splitting off of the recruitment of struggles like gender and race on the side of identity rather than on the model of class.

We don't have to see gender and race struggles as identity struggles at all.

So how does this relate to now then? The success of the rising Right, UKIP, Trump as well... It's no accident. Did I see the other day that Trump is giving Nigel Farage a job?[9] *(Laughter.)* Is that right? It makes sense though, because it's the same kind of strategy, in which you play class politics in order to suppress class consciousness. You appeal to the resentment of working-class people. I think the trope is always, *it's not us, it's them*, or *it's not you, it's them that's the problem*, and then that doubles to be a racialised argument. So, I think you've got an anti-articulation of class and race, you could say. They bring class and race together in order to negate the transformative potentials of both. You think class and race together in order to suppress the possibilities of race and class consciousness developing, or certainly in order to stop a sort of group consciousness developing whereby race and class were properly articulated.

Because it's not as if class consciousness is opposed to a consciousness based on race. It does *seem* that way, in the actual social world, but, of course, a true class consciousness would include all races, right? It wouldn't say only certain kinds of race really belong to this class and others don't. The point of a true class consciousness is its pan- nature. It covers all of them.

So, from the Right's point of view, that's exactly what must be avoided, right? That's exactly the kind of consciousness you do not want to see developing, a consciousness of that type. So, you can see it the other way round. OK, what kind of consciousness would we want developing? One that would recognise the ways in which these different kinds of subordination, exploitation, etc.

work together in order to maintain the status quo? But we have to overthrow that. The conditions for a real group consciousness developing would be the overthrowing of those kinds of divisions.

So, the racialised other is one part of it, which we can see with Trump and which we can see with UKIP. I think the other part of the Right is a form, then, of deflective class resentment, as we saw. It's not aimed against the richest. It's certainly not aimed against capital as the producer of class difference in the first place. It's aimed against professionals. And, in the context of the US in particular, I think, what we see is that there's perceived to be this alliance between professionals and the racialised other. So, the professional class means that the racialised other gets specialised treatment that you don't get. "You" being the WWC — the White Working Class.

So, I think that's the negative deflection that we can see in the present moment and in this text. There was the possibility of exactly this articulation of struggles, this proliferation of entry points, into a vision of a transformed new world. But they were deflected. They were turned back on themselves. Those potentials were blocked and real historical changes occurred, which meant that conditions shifted. One of which, as I said, was the recession.

What is described by Cowie, then, is partly arriving at conditions of relative prosperity. The Sixties' work conditions subverted prosperity. And, given the strength of existing unions, this allowed demands to become even more emboldened, stronger, and to make the shift into the qualitative. When the recession arrived, that strips organised labour of a lot of its power, particularly in [light of] conditions of recent automation, as you mentioned earlier.

So, we start to have the kind of lineaments, the picture

of a world that we have to navigate. So you see the rise in unemployment, automation, the decline of class power, and [Cowie] says, as you were mentioning earlier, this turn towards the so-called "Me Decade", this culture of individualism — the so-called "culture of narcissism", as described by Christopher Lasch, although for Lasch, in lots of ways, this undermines our sense of the individual, but we'll leave that for the moment.[10]

The power of the text then, for me, is that it opens up this vision of a potential route into postcapitalism. What if this *hadn't* happened? What if these countervailing forces hadn't managed to assert themselves in the Seventies? What if, instead, this new alliance of workers, the counterculture, etc., had come together in a sustained way? What if the demands about the quality of work had ultimately turned into demands for the abolition of work? These, for me, are some of the key questions posed by this insurgency, this moment, this breakout.

So, in lots of ways, in that period from the late Sixties into the early Seventies, we were as close as we were going to be to postcapitalism, to a transition into postcapitalism. We weren't going to get as close again, possibly, until now... Although now doesn't look very promising, does it?

Part of the question we can ask ourselves is: what are the conditions that led to these struggles in the late Sixties and early Seventies? Were they so specific that they can't be repeated? Or were they, in fact, something which we could imagine occurring again, and better?

What if there was no 1973? What if there was no recession? What if there was no retreat from these possibilities? What if the conservative backlash had not developed? Could we imagine this shift to postcapitalism having occurred? The other way of looking at it is, if that's the case, how do we get back to something like those conditions again in the current moment?

Perhaps we should also stress something that's only in the background of this text, and really in the background of this course, but which I'd like to bring to the foreground, which is the question of aesthetics. Is it an accident that this occurs at the end of the Sixties and the beginning of the Seventies — in aesthetic and cultural terms, you could say?

(*Silence.*)

OK. Sorry, it wasn't a rhetorical question, but I'll sort of answer it.

I'll say: It wasn't an accident. Partly what carried those energies was the force of the counterculture, and the counterculture then was primarily driven through music — but not exclusively. And that music, as much as politics, you could say, offered this vision of a liberated world. There was this kind of positive feedback loop in place. Music would feed into the struggles; the struggle would feed back into the music. And this was one sort of vector for the dynamics of transformation of the social world. And, of course, it's no accident then — particularly in the context of the US, if we're talking about that — that US music culture was driven by... A lot of the force behind that was black and working class.

We also have to bear in mind the weirdness of the US, given the situation around race. The Civil Rights struggle had only recently succeeded [in getting] legal recognition of black people [as equal citizens within society]... That legal recognition, as we can see today, is not always adhered to by any means. That's why it needs something like Black Lives Matter as a corrective. The fact is that the practice in everyday life is the non-recognition of black lives; the idea that black lives don't matter as much as white lives.

OK, so we've just had the legal acknowledgement of equality, at the same time as, throughout the Sixties, before anything happened, there was a popular culture dominated by black performers. So, the culture leads the way first, in lots of ways. That's one way that we can think of the aesthetic challenge and the political challenge. That's one thing that the counterculture is, you could say: some way of connecting those two things. And again, this is probably what we don't have now, right?

Let's not get into this... We've got Thirties, Seventies, now... Hang on, my maths is really bad. Thirties to Seventies is forty years. Forty years from the Seventies would go 2010 so, yeah, we kind of are there now. OK, that's good. So, there's a nice sort of symmetry to that. Thirties, Seventies, now. Yeah.

So, to be crude about it, schematically, in the Thirties there was this strong assertion of class power that didn't quite yield a revolution, and where, in which, the awareness of other forms of oppression, besides class exploitation, were not as strong. In the Seventies, there is a growing awareness of those [other] forms of struggle and oppression, and it is partly that that awareness takes expression in a counterculture. And the counterculture is not just a counter-politics; it's a range of forms of cultural expression.

And partly, as you said actually, there is the division between youth and the older generation. But that was probably, ultimately, problematic, that division between the youth and the older generation, and precisely became a means of dividing people rather than bringing them together. That's one of the things that meant McGovern couldn't do so spectacularly against Nixon in '72. He said, "look at these young freaks, you're not like them". *You.* Who is "you"? Well, it's some middle-aged, middle American person. It's always phantasmatic, you could say.

There isn't really a middle. But, nevertheless, the middle functions practically as this form of anti-consciousness. And that was partly an aim for the counterculture, which could define itself against this phantasmatic middle. But this was also problematic, you could say, in terms of building up a strong enough force to achieve hegemonic domination, hegemonic control of a society.

Anyway, that's something I'd like to think of going forward then: the cultural dimensions. How does the bourgeois culture, that the counterculture plays in, allow us to imagine a completely transformed world? That's what I'm suggesting, I guess, in terms of what we saw with black performers in the US. Their success preceded the actual shifts in racial dynamics in US society. Again, not that they were resolved, by any means, but culture allows this kind of performative anticipation of a radically transformed world.

But what kind of culture does allow that? And what kind of culture can sustain it? That's also the question we can really start to ask. The key thing is not to restrain activists towards some ideal realised utopia where everything works out. It failed. It went wrong. There were moments of rupture. There were glimmers. There was a sense of something that could have been different. But it didn't work out that way. Rather, the tremors that were felt at that time were transformed precisely, you could say, into cultural artefacts. What was left over were the cultural artefacts, which could then become some cooled-down commodities and sold as something to be individually consumed. That is always part of the dialectical nature of the culture of a transformational period. In one sense, it's feeding into a struggle, in another sense it's providing the conditions for a future commodification. And particularly, with the Sixties counterculture now, what is left are a series of commodified relics — the relics of what went into this struggle dimension becomes part of the nostalgic packaging around the commodity, that no longer features as... It's never going to see any light. The condition of our access to a commodity now is that we accept the struggle is something that has already happened, that has disappeared.

Partly, that is to do with this role that we can talk about, this new "mood" that Cowie talks about. What is a mood? It's a culture shift — a cultural shift towards individualism and the "Me Decade", thinking in terms of "I", thinking in terms of choice — individual choice — rather than collective transformation, etc.

What are the conditions that led to that? We've already looked at some of the conditions which led to that. And they have to be continually maintained, you could say.

Let's look at it this way: How do you have both someone thinking in terms of... In some sense belonging to a certain kind of identity — so you could say the identity of the White Working Class — yet also think of themselves as individuals? I've sort of already given the answer. It's partly by deflecting class into identity. So, as I said, identity then becomes a matter of a set of positive properties that we know and possess, and how we make that commensurate with individual identity is we deflect the attention away from common interests and common struggle[s] into a dimension of individual subjectivity. We all share certain positive characteristics as belonging to this class identity, but we can develop our own subjectivity in our own way within that. We're not defined by common interests and we're not defined by the overcoming of our current situation via a development of these common interests.

I'm trying to draw [out] the consequences of this story now. I'm trying to treat it as a kind of parable. How have we ended up in this situation that he describes? This kind of disillusion? [This] "individual withdrawal and sporadic rebellion bubbling forth from the simmering pot of daily conflict".[11]

As close as we'd been to this constellation of new forces to overcome society, by the end we were in this situation of radical dispersal, de-energisation, disillusion, solipsism, withdrawal, etc. That's a dramatic flip-round, in the period of a few years. Sometimes, the peak of these troubles, in the early Seventies, quickly preceded their immediate dissipation.

Partly I have to include this [text] also because I wanted the libidinal dimension of it to come into play. The question of desire, or rather... I think libido is different from desire. Libido is not only *what* we want but *why* we want it. The object causes it, in that sense. And what is raised by this? These struggles are articulated through the counterculture as the production of new forms of desire. We talked about this when we started off [in the first lecture]. I talked about the co-option of those forms of desire, via Apple, etc., which precisely individualises, which transforms all desire into a desire to be a more successful individual, etc. What is also raised here, then, is the spectre of a different kind of desire, a different kind of libido, a desire for a transformed world. You could say that the cultural expressions, in some sense, although they fed into the political struggles, were in many ways stronger than the actual political struggles were capable of being. That's precisely why, in some ways, they were able to survive the political struggles and were able to be retrospectively commodified after the event.

STUDENT #7: Sorry, could you repeat that last sentence?

MF: I'm not sure if I can! (*Laughter.*) What was I saying?

It was precisely because they were so potentially transformative that they could be so retrospectively commodified. Because the energy of transformation then becomes a kind of residual libido. When the conditions for the struggle are no longer there you can still appeal to that libido, the transformational libido. Which it still endlessly has to. Capital is always going on about the "revolutionary". The word "revolution" is a key commodity identifier now... You're sort of looking at me blankly... Don't you see this quite a lot? The word "revolution" used as a commodity? Names of restaurants, that kind of thing?[12] This appeal to dynamic flux, shift, creativity, all of that, is a key feature of advertising. This is kind of the argument of Boltanski and Chiapello in *The New Spirit of Capitalism*. I say that — you may not have read it. It was an important text for a lot of these discussions. It was very big — way too big for what was necessary — but a lot of their argument is really about how the counterculture became subdued, transformed, turned into... It wasn't simply defeated, it was incorporated into the core structure of capitalism now, which then has to be about creativity, self-reinvention, etc. etc. So the counterculture becomes mirrored in the current form of capitalism. So it doesn't simply *defeat* this stuff, it metabolises it, it absorbs it, it transforms it for its own ends. And that's what we can start to look at next week with Lyotard.

There is a tension — a potentially productive tension — between desire and Marxism. "The desire *named* Marx". What is the desire *within* Marxism? What is the role of libido, what is the role of desire, within the working class? What Lyotard suggests, scandalously, is that there was a desire for capital[ism] among the working class. And this is surely the key thing. To what extent do people *want* capitalism? Conversely, to what extent do people want postcapitalism? If desire is monopolised by capital, as we suggested at the start, then... that's it then, isn't it? The changes we need are never going to happen. Or rather, we have this vision of a kind of political project, on the one hand, and desire on the other, so that, in order to achieve this political project, we'll have to subdue our own desires. And that is highly problematic, I would suggest.

Maybe it's the converse of what we see in some of this countercultural stuff. Some of the countercultural stuff would say *we only need desire*. I guess this was what happened in 1972 with the election around McGovern. The forces of desire for counterculture were saying, *well, we don't need organised labour*. Organised labour is saying, *well, we don't need the forces of desire. We don't need that. That's disruptive. That will undermine the unity and resolute will and the organisational capacity of the existing labour institutions*. That tension, that failure to bring those two things together, I think, was part of the narrative that I want to take from today. There was some sense of that. That's what I like about it. There was some sense that you could have organised labour and countercultural libido *together*, for a moment. That was possible, [if] only in some temporary way at the time. What I'm suggesting is, then, that postcapitalist desire is a sustaining of that interlinking, that articulation.

We'll shift back into theory next week, which is easier but harder.

I forgot to ask someone to introduce the text this week, so can someone introduce Lyotard for us next week? *(Student raises their hand.)* Yeah? Anybody else want to have a go from a different angle? OK, just [student] then.

OK, thanks everybody.

Lecture Five:
Libidinal Marxism

5 DECEMBER 2016

MARK FISHER: OK, what did you make of Lyotard? [Student], I know you're introducing it, but what did other people make of the text?

STUDENT #1: Difficult.

MF: You thought it was difficult? OK. You thought it was more difficult than anything we've done so far? Maybe not more than the Lukács...

STUDENT #1: Yeah. I don't know...

MF: It's a loaded question...

STUDENT #1: I just felt like I got quite lost in it...

MF: OK, did anyone else feel that way...?

(*General chatter.*)

STUDENT #1: I couldn't figure out if he was being sarcastic or...

MF: OK, well I've highlighted some quotations we can go through, but let's hear first what [student] said.

(Here a student reads aloud a long introduction, summarising some of the concepts and peculiarities within Lyotard's text — his thrust towards the "intensities" and affects within Marx's writings; his almost Derridean wrestling with and description of a dichotomous textual Marx, who is at once an Old Man theorist and an amorous Little Girl, which transforms Marxism into "a strange bisexual assemblage".

Referred to by Lyotard himself as his "evil book", Libidinal Economy reads, at once, like a deeply theoretical and complex text and like a work of transgressive and erotic literature, as he channels a Bataillean view of Marxism from within the midst of 1970s post-structuralism. This strange relationship between styles and genres of philosophy and writing is part of what makes Lyotard's text so difficult and so enthralling.)

MF: It's a really difficult text and I think you've done well to pull out some of the big questions.

Let's get to what I see as the heart of this... or certainly what I think of as the key challenges that are posed and will be taken up by some of the later texts within the module — and that is the sections — the main paragraph from page 111, and the paragraph beginning on page 115.

But, you will say, it gives rise to power and domination, to exploitation and even extermination. Quite true; but also to masochism; but the strange bodily arrangement of the skilled worker with his job and his machine, which is so often reminiscent of the *dispositif* of hysteria, can also produce the extermination of a population: look at the English proletariat, at what capital, that is to say *their labour*, has done to their body. You will tell me, however, that it was that or die. *But it is always that or die*, this is the law of libidinal economy, no, not the law: this is its provisional, very provisional, definition in the form of the cry, of intensities of desire; 'that or die', i.e. that and dying from it, death always in it, as its internal bark, its thin nut's skin, not yet as its *price*, on the contrary as that which renders it unpayable. And perhaps you believe that 'that or die' is an *alternative*?! And that if they choose that, if they become the slave of the machine, the machine of the machine, fucker fucked by it, eight hours, twelve hours, a day, year after year, is it because they are forced into it, constrained, because they cling to life? Death is not an alternative to it, it is a part of it, it attests to the fact there is *jouissance* in it, the English unemployed did not become workers to survive, they — hang on tight and spit on me [**MF**: *I love that! (Laughter.)*] — *enjoyed* the hysterical, masochistic, whatever exhaustion it was of *hanging on* in the mines, in the foundries, in the factories, in hell, they enjoyed it, enjoyed the mad destruction of their organic body which was indeed imposed upon them, they enjoyed the decomposition of their personal identity, the identity that the peasant tradition had constructed for them, enjoyed the dissolution of their families and villages, and enjoyed the new monstrous *anonymity* of the suburbs and the pubs in the morning and evening.[1]

OK, I think this could be an epigraph for the course in a way — certainly for certain aspects of the course — the questions around accelerationism have a lot to do with this — and this brings up the relation of desire and capitalism. Is it the case simply that capitalism is imposed on the peasant body as something wholly unpleasant or is it something which engenders its own desire, or, as he puts it here, "forms of endurance"? And he wants to say: *no, it does! There are these forms of endurance intrinsic to capitalism!* The proletariat, then, is not the same as the peasantry here. The proletariat — the industrial proletariat — is something produced, partly, in this enjoyment of the dissolution of the old world.

What's key to this, then, is something that really goes throughout the chapter, which is overthrowing any notion of an outside to capital, repeatedly. That's the move that keeps being made. This is the move against Baudrillard, for instance. We'll look at Baudrillard later. We'll look at [Baudrillard's 1976 text] *Symbolic Exchange and Death* later. Part of the argument there is... Well, Baudrillard is a kind of primitivist. So, what he's saying is — and like Lyotard, it's a form of Marxist argument — in some ways you could say Baudrillard is more of a Marxist than Lyotard, in that he retains the idea of a critique of equivalence. The idea is that, with Marx, what happens in capitalism is that everything is made equivalent. This is what capital is, right? *X* physical thing here equals a virtual quantity of capital. This is what it is to inject things into a capitalist system — and Baudrillard opposes this to what he calls "symbolic exchange". Symbolic exchange, as Lyotard professes here, partly comes from Mauss's theory of gift-exchange — Marcel Mauss — the idea of gift exchange, which was a study of certain practices of so-called primitive societies — practices of potlatch — anyone heard of this?[2] Yeah. Basically, it's a form of ritualistic gift-giving often with a latent (or not so latent) aggression to it, where you escalate and escalate the gifts that are given, sometimes to the point where you burn down the whole village as a "top that!"

The thing is, with gift-exchange, there is no equivalent. There is no law of equivalence. If I give you something and you respond with something else, what is the metric that would make those things equivalent? There isn't anything. This is what Baudrillard says. This is the logic of the gift. It has nothing to do with any kind of law of equivalence. This is, then, a part of primitive societies that can be completely contrasted with capitalism. But Lyotard really wants to reject any attempt to find an outside to capitalism. Either everything is primitive, or nothing is primitive. Either capitalism is itself primitive… There is no subversive region. There is nothing beyond the purview of capital. This is what he says on page 108 at the bottom:

> There is one thing, then, which makes us say: there is no primitive society, that is to say: there is no external reference, even if immanent, from which the separation of what belongs to capital (or political economy) and what belongs to subversion (or libidinal economy), can always be made, and cleanly; where desire would be clearly legible, where its *proper economy* would not be scrambled. And this should be clearly understood: 'scrambled' does not mean 'thwarted', tainted, by a foreign, evil instance. This is simply the problematic of alienation…[3]

And this is also what he's rejecting, right? The idea of alienation. The "phantasy of a non-alienated region", as he puts it.[4] These kinds of dualisms, whereby there is a pure subversive region — a primitive region untainted by capitalism. There are no such regions. There are no such spaces. This is a relentless message in this text. And I think it's not clear if he means there never were primitive societies in this way, or certainly not now — there is no access to anything that would function like that. And it would also mean that there is no revolutionary outside either.

It's striking, I think, to read this text. I've called it "libidinal Marxism" but it's not about a desire-revolution at all, actually. It's more of a scathing assault on what he regards as close partners, like Baudrillard, and the general tendencies of the Left.

So, this text came out, as you said, in 1974 — that's six years after May '68 — so a long time after those events — a long time after the stewing of those events... And surely that is what colours the tone of this text, then... For me, it's come two years before its time in lots of ways — as a response to '68 — or clearly as a response to *Anti-Oedipus* — *Anti-Oedipus* of Deleuze and Guattari, which can be seen as the great book of '68, codifying and translating into theoretical terms a lot of the events that happened in May '68.

I'm referring to May '68 as if you know what it is but I assume most of you do. It was a proto-revolutionary configuration in France with workers, students, joining together, spilling onto the streets, a feeling that revolution was imminent. It didn't work out that way. There was a backlash. The Right consolidated power, etc. Some people even say that the Right containing of what happened in May '68 was the beginning of or a building-towards the neoliberal order that came afterwards.

But *Anti-Oedipus* from Deleuze and Guattari, which I said, in a way, not having Deleuze and Guattari on the reading list was somewhat perverse in a certain way, but they're present in their absence... Deleuze and Guattari, then, bring into theory some of these alignments that occurred in '68: the idea of desire and revolution going together, the idea of the countercultural currents plus the Left. And the idea of a different kind of revolutionary subject — if the term "subject" is really appropriate there — as we'll see when we come to accelerationism, one of the most famous passages in *Anti-Oedipus* is the one where they reject the idea of being able to withdraw from capitalism. They [don't] talk about withdrawing from the world market and instead they talk about accelerating the process. It's a famously ambiguous passage. It's another attempt, after Marcuse and the Frankfurt school, to think Freud and Marx together. And, as with Marcuse, there is an attempt to think of desire or libido not necessarily as paired with discontent in civilisation. The great pessimism of Freud consists in that equation: the idea that, as far as there is civilisation, there is discontent because, as we looked at with Marcuse, desire will never be commensurate with the organisation of life that requires work. Work involves this kind of subduing of desire. All other repression follows from that.

OK. So, all of those... — Lyotard, Baudrillard, Marcuse, Deleuze and Guattari — can be seen as attempts to overthrow this, to rethink libido and its relationship to politics, and to rethink how our social field could look if it wasn't based on this inevitable accommodation [and blockage] between desire and work.

With Lyotard, I think, we still don't have this positive project so much in this — at least in this chapter, or anywhere, really — and there's a kind of interesting tendency of this text, right? Despite the fact he has a kind of sarcastic aside against Nietzsche at some point — it's quite a Nietzschean text, I think — and you can see the influence of Deleuze and Guattari. Part of the influence of Deleuze and Guattari is towards immanence — an emphasis towards immanence — towards a kind of flatness, towards this idea of there being only one plane, against dualism, against this idea of a split between... I guess against the idea of various kinds of splits — between the primitive and the modern, for instance — and also in terms of the rejection of critique, I think. The rejection of critique is also a kind of Nietzschean, Deleuzo-Guattarian move. The idea of thinking in terms of intensities in relation to zero — this is also kind of Deleuzo-Guattarian...

STUDENT #2: (*Inaudible question, presumably about one*

of Lyotard's strange and ambiguous concepts – "the Great Zero".)

MF: Yeah. I think it's a bit like when Deleuze and Guattari talk about the body without organs. It's the point of maximum potentiality, really, where rather than having presence and absence, you have zero and intensities in relation to zero. When Deleuze and Guattari talk about the body without organs, it's similar to that. This idea of something which is a kind of pure virtuality. It's an event against which we count up. You count up intensities in relation to it.

STUDENT #3: So, it's like a plateau?

MF: The zero? Yeah, that might be one way to think about it. But zero is just the way we think about zero. It's the point of an absence of anything actually existing. If you think about intensities on a scale — intensities of temperature or whatever — zero is both an absence of temperature, in a way, but it is also the referent against which... It's also a kind of temperature. Zero is a temperature. It's both a lack of temperature and the thing from which all other temperatures are counted up from and I think that's the way to think about zero.

STUDENT #4: And this is also the body without organs?

MF: Well, I think it's close to a body without organs, yeah.

STUDENT #4: So, it's about having that presence but without the...

MF: Yeah, so I think when things are zero, they are never allowed to...

STUDENT #2: *(Inaudible question, asking about more of Lyotard's peculiar concepts.)*

MF: Perhaps if we look at a particular section where he uses the word "zero". *(The whole class seems to scan the text, looking for a particularly pertinent example.)* It's not something I thought about this time when reading through...

STUDENT #3: If you want, I can read — in this book, there is a glossary...

MF: Oh yes, well, the glossary is about as complicated as the text itself...

STUDENT #3: ...And there is a definition of "The Great Zero". The Great Zero is "the name Lyotard gives to the instance informing a particular but insistent *dispositif* on the libidinal band".[5] And it also has another definition for the "libidinal band":

> ...the libidinal band is folded back into a theatrical volume which has an inside and an outside (appearance/ essence, signs/the signified). The inside is then ultimately considered in terms of what is going on on the outside. One of the most important figurations of the outside is the great Zero which serves as a general term to cover the Platonic world of forms, God, the authentic mode of production, the phallus, etc. All these instances — and despite their differences — are effects of the slowing down of the bar, referring to the intensities running through the band to an elsewhere which they appear to lack once they have been confined to the interiority of a volume. The great Zero is thus an empty centre which reduces the present complexity of what happens instantaneously on

the band to a 'chamber of presence and absence'. In his description of the great Zero Lyotard wishes to show that all theories of signification are fundamentally 'nihilistic'.[6]

(*Silence.*)

MF: Yes.

(*All laugh.*)

STUDENT #3: I think that the main quote — "the great Zero which serves as a general term to cover the Platonic world of forms, God, the authentic mode of production, the phallus" — this is the sign of the outside, maybe — the outside that Lyotard is against constantly... I don't know...

MF: Yes, I think that is a Deleuzo-Guattarian take on the Great Zero... Reading it that way, the Great Zero becomes something which is eschewed in all of these theories as this point of outside, where outside can be separated from inside. And all of this complicated machinery — which doesn't come that much into this chapter, actually — I was trying to avoid all this stuff on the libidinal band, etc. — because frankly I've never been able to follow it that closely. (*Laughs.*) But with the great Zero, it becomes a way of establishing an outside — so the outside, yeah, the authentic mode of production or the world of forms, etc. — something which would stabilize the tension between outside and inside, that's what it's trying to say...

What he's trying to posit, then, is a space without this distinction between inside and outside. He's both trying to account for where the appearance of inside and outside, and the distinction between appearance and reality itself.... He's trying to account for that, where that comes from, and also to account for how it doesn't really exist, ultimately. So, ultimately, there is only this single plane of intensities. This is the libidinal cartography that he tries to outline. However, there is also the sense that there is a distinction between the inside and outside, the transcendent and immanent, a space of how things currently are and a revolutionary outside. These things constantly keep appearing, but how? What are the mechanisms for these appearances? That's what he's ultimately trying to account for, in this rather complicated work.

STUDENT #2: In the introduction, the translator tries to speak clearly about how this [style of] language came about in the translation from French to English... *(Inaudible.)* But I think this text is very different to anything we've read so far... Because all of these claims that he makes about arguments get undone, but it's much harder to understand the argument than the final claims that he makes: the proletariat desires suffering. But I think he goes deep into semiotics and lots of other stuff to back up that point, and I don't understand half the argument.

MF: You don't understand the argument about the proletariat wanting...?

STUDENT #2: For example.

MF: OK, yeah.

STUDENT #2: Like that paragraph that we read. It takes itself as libidinal. It's passionate. You can connect to it.

But in the sense of the argumentation, I cannot connect to it. I cannot see through it and feel that this...

(Inaudible.)

MF: Yes...

The question is, is it an argument at all? That's partly my hesitation. To say it's an argument... You say there's an argument, but I wonder if "argument" is quite the right term for what happens in this text — and perhaps I "read it wrongly" in the sense of not necessarily reading it in terms of arguments at all. But in terms of...

Well, let's take it at face value. At face value, he's saying: "I'm not going to interpret Marx". He isn't going to interpret Marx. He's not going to critique Marx. He is instead — what's he going to do? — he's going to work with certain intensities in the Marxist text. And he's going to work with and against certain dominant ways of reading Marx, and of reading what is in Marx. And this is partly what is problematic... There's a problematic gendering that keeps coming up through the text, I think. It comes up first in this opposition between the Old Man Marx and the Little Girl Marx. What is the Old Man Marx?

STUDENT #3: A theorist? A writer?

MF: Yeah. He's a kind of writer-prosecutor figure. This is the Marx who is making the case against capital. *The Great Prosecutor Marx*. This is the first tension that we work with, and these are ways of drawing out certain tendencies within Marx[ism] itself... What is the Little Girl Marx, though? If Old Man Marx is the Prosecutor making a case against capital, what is the Little Girl Marx?

STUDENT #3: The part that is fascinated with capital? That is seduced by capital?

MF: I'm not... Is that right?... I don't think so. I think it's more that the Little Girl Marx is the...

STUDENT #4: The Marx that is offended by the perversity of capital? Another part of himself?

MF: Yeah. They're both Marx.

STUDENT #2: *(Inaudible question.)*

MF: Yeah, but... If we look at page 98:

> The young innocent Little Girl Marx says: you see, I am in love with love, this must stop, this industrial and industrious crap, this is what makes me anxious, I want to return to the (in)organic body; and it has been taken over by the great bearded scholar so that he may establish the thesis that *it cannot stop*, and so that he may testify, as the counsel to the poor (amongst which is the Little Girl Marx), to his revolutionary conclusions; so that he may give, *to her*, this *total body* he requires, this child, at least this child of words which would be the anticipated double (the younger child born first) of the child of flesh: of the proletariat, of socialism. But alas, he does not give her this child. She will never have this 'artistic whole' before her, these writings 'in their entirety'. She will have suffering growing before her and in her, because her prosecutor will discover in the course of his research, insofar as it is endless, a strange *jouissance*: the same *jouissance* that results from the instantiation of the pulsions and their discharge in *postponement*.[7]

I think there is the key opposition. She wants it to be over. And this is, as I said, part of the series of problematic genderings throughout the text. The Little Girl Marx is kind of naive. The Little Girl Marx just doesn't like capitalism and wants it to be over with. Whereas the Old Man Marx is making the case against capitalism, and together they should have this child which should be the revolutionary subject of the proletariat. But this child never comes, because the Old Man Marx is never done with the prosecution of the case against capital.

This thing about deferring. Don't come yet. Never come. The case is never finalised.

STUDENT #4: Which Lyotard associated with his writing...

MF: Yes, so Marx's writing is never finished, right?[8]

That's one of the cryptic, the driving... It's a comment on Marx's work. It's more about the case against capital than it is about completing that case. And that is partly about the shifting to praxis, rather than the theoretical case against capital. There is some sort of complicity between Marx making the case against capital and capital itself.

STUDENT #2: So he's saying that Marx — or Marxism — *enjoys* capitalism and not finishing it because then he would lose its culture of critique?

MF: Yes, I think so. That's part of it. His endless deferring in getting rid of the object of critique [means that] at the same time... the critique is never finished. The critique is never finished, which means that the work of getting rid of capital can never really start. And the other way round, right?

STUDENT #2: What is the agency of this Little Girl, then?

MF: Well, they're part of the same thing, in some way, aren't they? That's the other thing. They're part of this unstable body that is not a whole. This is the other thing about the "(in)organic", right? The body which has a desire to return to some wholeness. There is no wholeness. There is no undivided body. I guess that means there is no nature. There is no pure realm. There is no pure, uncorrupted realm. There are only split, incommensurate bodies which cannot be added up into a kind of wholeness or unity. Ever. Marx himself then becomes another example of this kind of body, in this region.

STUDENT #5: Does Little Girl Marx also represent the dream of revolution within his writing as well?

MF: That's the way that I would understand it. But it's a kind of naive dream, isn't it? *Let's be done with it. It's all over.*

It seems to me that the key claim, which is also repeated — and this would be part of the argument, insofar as there is one — this notion of [there being] no outside. There isn't just one plane of intensities on which there are monstrous bodies of various kinds, defined by their affects, defined in terms of their affects and intensities, rather than their surface and depth and volume, as if there is some kind of surface beneath which there is a deeper appearance which can be understood — instead of that, look at bodies, intensities, affects [in themselves]... This is key.

Surely the message, then, throughout the chapter, is that there is no outside of this. So, the proletariat cannot be assigned to a position of the outside. He doesn't want a distinction between inside and outside at all.

The distinction between inside and outside is [a kind of] problematic theatre representation that he is trying to overcome with this model of intensities and affects.[9]

One way of looking at [the proletariat] is as a purely artificial entity, then. But, in a way, everything is artificial because there is no nature. The idea of nature as opposed to culture would be re-inscribing these distinctions which he is endlessly trying to undercut throughout this chapter.

> For what happens to whomever does not want to recognize that political economy is libidinal, is that he reproduces in other terms the same phantasy of an externalized region where desire would be sheltered from every treacherous transcription into production, labour and the law of value. The fantasy of a non-alienated region.[10]

This is what he says on page 107. "The fantasy of a non-alienated region": this is what I take this to be about, and one of the things I strongly take away from this chapter. *There is no non-alienated region*, at all. So, if we're looking for a postcapitalist politics — and I'm not sure how hard Lyotard is looking for that at this stage...

Lyotard had been involved in various left-wing groups, some of which he spits down at in passing during this chapter, but I think at this point he is pretty much in a state of misanthropic rejection of actually-existing left-wing positions. So, I see this as not really putting forward a positive programme for political transformation at all. That's probably why he called it a libidinal Marxism. What it's posing is a problem. If this is the case — if there is no subversive region — if we stick with the fantasy of a non-alienated region, then how are we to articulate what a transformational politics might be or could be? That's what I take to be at least the core of this, beneath all the specific difficulties of the text, the complexities of argument...

STUDENT #3: If, as Lyotard contends, there is no subversive region... There is no alternative. So Lyotard is a capitalist realist.

MF: No, I don't think he's saying that. What he's saying is, surely, that we can't conceive of a beyond, in terms of a radical outside, which has nothing in common with where we are now. Isn't that more what is being suggested, rather than we have to give in to capital?

STUDENT #3: So, the alternative is *inside* capitalism, more or less? We have to find an alternative *within* capitalism.

MF: I don't think that's quite right. I don't know what other people think, having read this. I don't think he's saying that...

STUDENT #3: No, I'm not saying that's what Lyotard is saying. But if there is no outside and we can find an alternative, so the alternative has to be inside... Or has to depart from inside...

STUDENT #6: Isn't it like an accelerationist...

STUDENT #3: Yes, I'm thinking of that.

MF: Yeah, it surely paved the way for that... There is no beyond that is untainted by capital, which is different from saying that things always have to be as they are now. The implicit message, surely, is that we have to imagine a transformation *out of* where we are now. We can't fall for any temptation to look for an untainted region, a non-alienated region, etc. We have to start from a full immersion in capital.

STUDENT #2: When it comes to finding a way through this text, and how we might or might not give in to alternative ways and stuff — his distinction from Deleuze and Guattari, I think, is important to understand. I don't fully understand it, but because it is important to see how Lyotard is differently contributing to the accelerationist agenda — different, as I say, from Deleuze and Guattari — because this idea of making our way from the within of capitalism, by ways of intensifying the immanent — that's not like them.

MF: Yeah, that's not like them.

STUDENT #2: So, it's important to see how he is not like them... (*Laughs*)

MF: Yeah, as far as I can see, that consists in the fact that he retreats from any positive project in relation to this, doesn't he? At least in relation to this chapter. With Deleuze and Guattari, they're prepared to talk about revolution and revolutionary power, but they just want to think of it in ways that are different from traditional Marxist ways of understanding that — or certainly different from these models that would posit a complete outside of capital.

It's partly this whole drama of alienation. This whole way of thinking in terms of alienation and non-alienation — rejecting all of that and thinking in terms of, partly, intensities and tendencies, right? Accelerating tendencies.

But one difference, for me, between *Anti-Oedipus* and [*Libidinal Economy*] is that there is a positive tendency there [in *Anti-Oedipus*]. There isn't a positive programme here. Maybe I've failed to detect it. I don't know what others thought. For me, it's maybe a kind of diagnostic exercise; a literary diagnostic exercise. He's reading Marx *as a writer*. It's, in some sense, a literary reading. He's drawing out the tropes, the metaphors, the conceptual figures in Marx and, rather than commenting on them, he's forming them through his own kind of literary dreamworld. That's what this is, with this complicated machinery around libidinal bands, zeroes, all this kind of stuff.

That's why Lyotard's text seems, in a way, more modern than *Anti-Oedipus*, because of its lack of a... Because it seems to really fit into that moment, really, after the Sixties, after the Seventies, when this clearly has become the problem: the immersion into capital, the lack of any outside, or the difficulty of thinking of the working class now as separate from and outside capital. And particularly in terms of this question of desire, which we looked at at the start [in the first lecture], with the examples of Levi's jeans, etc. Which would be another version of this, right? That Levi's thing. There is no outside. There is no Soviet realm where people don't want Levi's. We're talking about sausage pâtés and all of that here. The proletariat want these sausage pâtés in the same way they want Levi's. But he doesn't really seem to have an answer to this problem. It's more like, *this has to be faced*. This has to be recognised. And where do we go from there? I don't think he has the answer to that, does he?

STUDENT #3: No.

STUDENT #7: I don't know. Perhaps I'm not reading this

correctly but, towards the end of the text, I think there is this sort of shift in tone? And this is towards the very end, on pages 148 and 149, where he sort of does provide a couple of — not exactly solutions but — slightly more positive notions, where he starts talking about... First, he talks about Marx's idea of the extension of leisure time and the reduction of working time and then there's an interesting passage... I don't know, maybe I'm just misreading it.

MF: Maybe not!

STUDENT #7: Yeah, OK, I'm just going to read a couple of sentences.

MF: Tell us where it is?

STUDENT #7: It's at the end of 148 and then the first couple of sentences of 149:

And the formation of additional capital, you are well aware that it has become impossible legitimately to impute to it the metaphysical difference between the use-value and the exchange-value of an alleged labour-force, a difference which alone would be at the origin of surplus-value; but what if in general it would require simply an inequality or a difference of potential somewhere in the system, a difference which marks its frame at the same time as it attests that this system could not be isolated, what if it must ceaselessly draw from new reserves of energy in order to transform them *into more commodities*. Perhaps it 'had to' draw initially on human energy, but this is not essential to it, and it can survive exploitation quite well, in the sense that you, the prosecutor for the poor, understand it, and requires, like every other complex natural system, only an irreversible superiority in its metabolic relation with the bio-physico-chemical context from which it draws its energy.[11]

Because before he was undertaking this critique — even though I don't think you would call it a critique — of these abstract formulas of how surplus-value is produced — you know, labour-force exchange-value — and he wanted to distance himself from these abstract notions and bring forth this idea of libidinal intensities behind all this. And then he says that these libidinal intensities, maybe, at the beginning, had to come, at first, from human energy, but that is not essential to it.

Maybe I'm just misreading, but it is a sort of accelerationist moment here. I think these are his most accelerationist couple of passages, where he points at these libidinal intensities in capital that can come from humans but also from somewhere else, like from machines. And on the page before — or the pages after — I think there is a passage where he does mention technology and mechanisation, and that that can be another source for these libidinal intensities.

I don't know. Maybe this is just a misreading.

MF: I don't think it's a misreading, but I think it highlights, for me, one of the difficulties of the text. Is this still some kind of reading of Marx? Or is it a model for a political programme? Do you know what I mean?

STUDENT #7: Yeah, it's hard to separate what's his idea and what's his reading of Marx, I think.

MF: Yeah, and what is also his putting-into-play of

certain kinds of tropes or quasi-literary figures coming out of Marx, etc., etc.

But yes, I think you're right, that could be one potential programme there.

OK. I've highlighted some other passages which might be worth going over. But I think my error here — my motivation for choosing the text, in a way, which might be in error — is seeing it as posing this set of problems rather than making a careful set of arguments. In a way, I think a lot of what he's saying — this is what I mean about what makes it modern — would be self-evident precisely in the era of capitalism realism. The things that he's arguing [for] start to become self-evident. But in the Seventies, maybe, people could appeal to the idea of a primitive society as a source of overcoming capitalism. How do we think about overcoming capitalism? Well, maybe, like Baudrillard, you look to primitive societies and they have forms of ritualised gift-exchange as an alternative to it. Maybe you look for some radical space outside. But I think, by the Nineties — and I think this was translated [into English] in the Nineties — it's very significant. By that time, there isn't really any sense that this [possibility of primitivist retreat] is the case.

Is there an argument for this? These claims are kind of foundational, aren't they? They seem to be somewhat foundational. There is no primitive society, which is the same as every political economy is libidinal. I don't know if he argues for this. Does he? That is the basis of everything that he's saying... Perhaps I'm wrong in the way I'm reading it.

STUDENT #2: What would be the function of all those paragraphs... talking about signs and symbolic exchange and about the foundation of Baudrillard's thought...?

What are those paragraphs doing? I don't understand those paragraphs fully...

I was also thinking about [Srnicek and Williams'] *Inventing the Future*, the text that we read in the very first session. Should we look at all those proposals and arguments? Because those proposals are very well argued in that book. Should we think that those are looking quite naive in the face of this? How powerfully does this persist up to this day? Can we think of, for example, proposals hidden in *Inventing the Future* — or accelerationism in general — having its way through this kind of pessimism and nihilism?

MF: The question of pessimism and nihilism is very interesting in relation to this text, because he's always wanting to reject critique and negativity. Be on the side of affirmation. That's what I meant about this Nietzschean thing. It's like Nietzsche in the sense that Nietzsche is always going on about affirming but always attacking things. Lyotard is sort of doing that, isn't he? He rejects critique but all he seems to do is critique. And that's this kind of intricate argument... The intricate engagements with Baudrillard...

But secondly, I would say that *Inventing the Future* is really about the problems that this poses. The problem of [there being] no easy access to an outside, no readily apparent already-existing space that is untainted by capital... But it's a very different kind of text, though, isn't it? I think that's part of the issue. Part of the difficulty of [*Libidinal Economy*] is the different levels of it, one of which, as I say, is the readings of readings — his own kind of literary figuration. His literary figuration and the way he constructs these different kinds of figures... He wouldn't want to call them metaphorical... Metaphorical confections... But let's go with that for the moment. He's just doing all of that. It's very different from a kind of straightforwardly programmatic text about *what do we change, how do we do it, how do we invent the future...* But the relation would be that Lyotard is posing the problem that *Inventing the Future* is starting to answer, and it's posing the problem in terms of... I'm not sure he can answer this himself, at all, even if he wants to — the kind of problems he's presenting us with... But he's trying to point to the insufficiencies of all these other theories as he sees them.

STUDENT #4: There's one part that I think is very interesting. My sense of this text was pretty much about systems of signification and how they cannot truly exist, in a way. This is particularly true when he points to Lacan. He says: "When Lacan says: to love is to give what one has not, he means: to forget that one is castrated".[12] And then he goes and talks about the affects in Lacan and Lacan's "theory of communication, that carries with it the entire philosophy of the subject, the philosophy of the body haunted by self-appropriation and property since the theory of communication is obviously just a piece of economic theory".[13] For me, then, I read this as everything comes down to numbers. (*Laughs.*)

MF: It comes down to numbers?

STUDENT #4: Well, he's signifying — there's a lot of intensity in what he's saying...

MF: I think it comes down to intensities, this model, rather than signifiers. Signifiers would be relational in the classic ways analysed by [Ferdinand de] Saussure, whereas intensities are about degrees, aren't they? So, signifiers have their meaning in relation to other signifiers. Intensity has a quantity... It's about quantity, isn't it? Rather than about numbers as such... Does that make sense? Intensities are "intensive quantities", to use a phrase from Deleuze and Guattari.[14] He's wanting to move things onto that level, rather than the pathos of absence and presence that you get with signifiers in the post-structuralist analysis of signifiers and the signified.

But that's a separate problem. Concentrating on this capital stuff, let's look at some passages. On [page] 113:

> Finally, you must also realize that such *jouissance*, I am thinking of that of the proletariat, is not at all exclusive of the hardest and most intense *revolts. Jouissance* is *unbearable.* It is not in order to regain their dignity that the workers will revolt, break the machines, lock up the bosses, kick out the deputies... There are libidinal positions, tenable or not, there are positions invested which are immediately disinvested, the energies passing onto other pieces of the great puzzle, inventing new fragments and new modalities of *jouissance*, that is to say of intensification. There is no libidinal dignity, nor libidinal fraternity, there are libidinal contacts without communication...[15]

Again, I see this as a rejection of a certain kind of appeal, and a certain tone of leftist discourse.

"*Jouissance*" — the Lacanian term, also theorised by Barthes — *jouissance*, libido, versus dignity.

[Page] 114 — this sentence is on quantity again:

> How many iron bars, tonnes of sperm, decibels of carnal shrieks and factory noises, more and still more: this *more* may be invested as such, it is in capital, and it must be recognized that not only is it completely inane, we fully accept this, it is no more nor less vain than either

political discussion on the *agora* or the Peloponnesian war, but it is especially necessary to recognize that this is not even a matter of production. These 'products' are not products, what counts here, in capital, is that they are endured, and endured *in quantity*; it is the quantity, the imposed number that is itself already a motive for intensity, not the qualitative mutation of quantity, not at all, but as in Sade the frightening number of blows received, the number of postures and manoeuvres required, the necessary number of victims...[16]

Quantity itself is a motivator, a producer of intensity. And this is part of the sadomasochistic reading of capital and the proletariat that he tries to outline in this chapter. With the proletariat there is a masochistic desire. There is an enjoyment of being subjugated to the intensities of capital.

Capital can be understood in this sadistic sense... A quantity of intensities, and the quantity itself becomes significant. The quantity is not just over and on top of what is actually happening. It is itself a motivation for the events.

Another section — [pages] 115–116. This is [Lyotard] supposing the problem that we face today. This is the sausage pâté section. (*Laughter.*)

Why, political intellectuals, do you *incline towards* the proletariat? In commiseration for what? I realize that a proletarian would hate you, you have no hatred because you are bourgeois, privileged smooth-skinned types, but also because you dare not say the only important thing there is to say, that one can enjoy swallowing the shit of capital, its materials, its metal bars, its polystyrene, its books, its sausage pâtés, swallowing tonnes of it till you burst — and because instead of saying this, which is *also* what happens in the desire of those who work with their hands, arses and heads, ah, you become a leader of *men*, what a leader of *pimps*, you lean forward and divulge: ah, but that's alienation, it isn't pretty, hang on, we'll save you from it, we will work to liberate you from this wicked affection for servitude, we will give you dignity. And in this way you situate yourselves on the most despicable side, the moralistic side where you desire that our capitalized's desire be totally ignored, forbidden, brought to a standstill, you are like priests with sinners, our servile intensities frighten you, you have to tell yourselves: how they must suffer to endure that! And of course we suffer, we the capitalized, but this does not mean that we do not enjoy, nor that what you think you can offer us as a remedy — for what? — does not disgust us, even more. We abhor therapeutics and its Vaseline, we prefer to burst under the quantitative excesses that you judge the most stupid. And don't wait for our spontaneity to rise up in revolt either.[17]

This is a great passage of writing!

I think, then, that the libidinal economy of this writing, of Lyotard himself, is largely to do with — not a relation to a specific political project but — a kind of hatred of almost all existing left-wing models of what political transformation entails. (This is probably a simplistic level at which I've taken the key message of the text.) These [left-wing projects] are all inadequate and all for the same reason, over and over again, in that they don't take the desire of the capitalized seriously. They reject it and are therefore keep re-inscribing moralism. And in re-inscribing moralism they keep re-invoking this distinction between inside and outside, between immanence and transcendence, between the realm of capital and a realm outside it, which would be pure and free from this.

But to be free from capital would be to be free from desire! Isn't this the problem that he keeps talking about? In order to understand capital, we don't only need Marx, we need to understand Marx alongside Sade.[18] That's that point about quantity — with Sade there are a thousand blows or whatever. He's making that analogy — or perhaps more than an analogy — between the quantificatory dimension of enjoyment in Sade and the quantities of the way that capital counts. He's continually insisting on this convocation of desire and capital.

STUDENT #2: Just to make sure that I understand: by breaking free from desire, this doesn't mean to withdraw from our capacity to desire but to let go of the distinction of what is the pleasure in desire and in suffering.

MF: Yes, I think that's right. I think that's important as well. That's important to draw out.

We have to throw aside a simple utilitarian model of desire, of pleasure. Utilitarian would be the idea that we move away from pain and we're motivated towards pleasure. We seek pleasure and we move to avoid pain. Anything from Sade to Freud… Particularly in Sade and Freud, I think, there is an attempt to express that this is not the case. There is a complicated attraction to what is painful. What is suffering can also be enjoyed. That's a good point. It's a really important point that I think is really implicit.

That has implications, right? The co-implication of suffering and desire would also pose a set of complicated questions, then, about capitalism, right? If capitalism makes you suffer but also you enjoy that suffering, what does that mean?

STUDENT #8: You're bound to it?

MF: Yeah, right. You're bound to it, but you're bound to it not only by its relation to the libido. There's the enjoyment of eating sausage pâtés and all that kind of thing, but there's also a libido of subjugation and of artificiality and of disillusion.

STUDENT #2: Isn't this precisely trying to get us not to think about the question you just asked? At least in a practical sense? I mean, [Lyotard] is very much trying not to write something that can be practically interpreted. This text is not like Marx's text, which was then translated into the practice of politics in the street. He doesn't want this to happen to his own text. I also think that this critique is fundamental to *Capital* in itself. He's trying to do that very same thing in his own text by making it manifest that everything ever written is a text, before being translated into anything more practical. We see this at the start of the chapter. This plane of intensities is the plane of writing itself. I saw this chapter about the "Economy of This Writing".[19] I didn't read it, but I assume...

MF: That's a good question as well. It raises interesting problems as well. If the plane of intensities is the writing... Does that make things, ultimately, *more* or *less* intense? Because it produces everything... In one sense you're saying that the writing is, then, (allegedly) purely immanent. The writing is not about something in itself. The writing is this swirl of intensities that has no deeper referent.

That intensifies the writing, but it also means it's *just* writing. It's not about anything. It's not moored to anything. It's just *text*, in a way, albeit a text of a particularly intense sort. There's a kind of doubleness, I think, there, in the background, that is a potentially interesting problem. But I think it highlights the problems, the impasses, of Lyotard's own desire.

Lyotard seems here... [He] has a gloriously hemmed-in quality. His rejection of more or less all other forms of leftism, his rejection of the transcendent function of theory — the idea of theory or writing separate from what it's writing about — ends up, then, in this series of negations or blockages, and this kind of self-circulating writing, or a self-justifying circulation of intensities, as he calls it. Is that a display of the glorious kind of autonomy and sufficiency of the text itself, or its impotence or uselessness? The fact that it cannot do anything beyond itself?

Oh gosh, we're nearly coming to the end...

What I wanted people to take from this was, really, those questions about the complication of desire and capitalism, particularly in that historical moment of the Seventies, [when we] really started to think desire as immanent to capitalism — not even to capitalism — immanent to work, a kind of capitalist desire that is immanent to a working class. What do we do about that? Do we reject it? Do we moralise about it? Or not?

Lyotard clearly thinks we shouldn't reject it, we shouldn't moralise about it, but I don't think he has a clear model of what the alternative to moralising about it would be. He seems to be suggesting that there must be a way of accounting for or dealing with this desire, at the very least. At some other level, it might even be more than that. It might be that we have to celebrate this desire.

Ultimately, then, what I'm reading this as, is to do with the impasses of leftist theory — but it is itself a more massive impasse. It is not offering a way out of this.

Partly because it has precluded this conclusion of a way out, by going on about "there is no subversive region", there's no outside...

So, where did this come from? What is it going towards? This is where we end up in a kind of performative nihilism, I think, even if he thinks it's not nihilistic. The text itself, even if we see it as a self-propelling circulation of intensities, as he wants [us] to, that itself seems quite nihilistic. What is the use of this beyond its own terms?

I suggest, then, that the use of it is a diagnostic one. It points to these impasses, points to these problems — problems that are still not solved and which pose all kinds of difficulties to this day. The old, simple model — alienation implies an unalienated world; the struggle to restore the unalienated world — this is the old model, which [Lyotard] rejects. We give that up. We say, let's give up the fantasy of the unalienated world, uncontaminated by capital. What are we left with? This is a confusing and difficult and either an overcomplete or incomplete answer to that question.

STUDENT #9: This might be a bit far-fetched, but maybe that's his suggestion... You spoke about Nietzsche and when Nietzsche says "there is no truth, there are only interpretations". So maybe Lyotard's suggestion of going beyond this would be getting rid of interpretations. He starts off — and I have to say that I wasn't able to read it as closely as I would have liked to — when he suggests that interpretations of Marx are like interpretations of the Bible, or whatever. And then we get into this [Derridean] realm of everything is text, and there's no beyond text, because interpretations are always texts, even though they are political practices.

And so the only way of getting beyond this — or maybe also at the same time when Foucault suggests, in "What is an Author?" — the two significant authors in this text are Marx and Freud because they have found this other discourse which means they basically created a new way of doing a text over and over and over again.

So Lyotard's suggestion might be that this should be the last text on Marx, because the definition of the [Great] Zero sounded very much like Deleuze's reading of Leibniz and the monad: the outside is the inside and keeps folding over and over again.[20] There is no fixed inside or outside because they keep changing all the time. And the outside can become the inside and the inside the outside, so this eventually means there's not an inside or an outside. So, getting rid of an outside and an inside, and of interpretation, would mean the start of getting beyond capitalism? That might be the idea? Not as proclaiming political practice or a solution to the problem, but maybe as suggesting a way to start getting to the resolving the problem?

MF: Yeah, it's interesting: the question of moving beyond interpretations as well as moving beyond truth. But there's always two levels to the text. He's gesturing towards... He's surely still offering interpretations but, instead of straightforward interpretations, he offers up his own literary figurations, doesn't he? Instead of, for instance, offering analysis of Marx's work, saying there's two tendencies in it, there's a tendency towards critique and there's a smaller tendency towards trying to completely break out of capitalism, he posits the Old Man Marx and the Little Girl Marx and all that stuff. That's not so much an interpretation as a *translation* of certain tendencies with Marx's writing into figures within Lyotard's writing, but it's still somewhat at the level of interpretation.

There's this fantasy of intensity, this fantasy of having

gotten away from this second real transcendent level, and to simply be operating on the level of quantitative intensities and not interpretations. Is that possible? And isn't this just a way of reading it?

It seems to me that it's not really possible, and that we're still, in some sense, in the realm of interpretation, just as we're still in the realm of critique. But the disavowal of critique and the disavowal of interpretation are interesting in their own right. It produces a different kind of writing.

(Exasperated.) OK, right. *(Laughter.)* I hope that something has got through.

Next time we've got some relatively easier stuff. Autonomia. Does anyone want to introduce Autonomia and the refusal of work after Christmas?

(Student volunteers.)

Yeah, it's quite short, so you can maybe read some other stuff.

Anyone want to do the Thoburn?

(Student volunteers.)

Does anyone else want a tutorial and they've not signed up for it?

(Silence.)

OK, so everyone else feels OK about what they're going to do for the essay, for January? Yeah? OK. You can always email me about it.

(General clattering and voices as the class leaves.)

Appendix One:
Course Syllabus

Following Mark Fisher's death on Friday, 13 January 2017, the remaining ten weeks of the "Postcapitalist Desire" seminar did not go ahead as intended.

For the first few weeks, students continued to use the seminar room during the module's scheduled Monday morning time slots to sit together and remember their lecturer. Later, as the weeks progressed, the decision was made to try and continue the course in Fisher's memory.

The seminar was transformed into a kind of reading group, with the help of a number of Fisher's friends, colleagues, collaborators, and influences being invited to join students in their discussions of the texts that Fisher had intended to explore.

These reconstructed sessions later turned into a more public reading group, under the title "Nothings Into Somethings", in which some of these same texts were discussed again in a more public forum.[1]

The titles and readings for the following ten sessions are included below, along with readings for the five sessions above. This syllabus reflects the original form, content and editions used by Fisher, provided on the contents page of the reader he produced for the course.

Lecture One: What is Postcapitalism?

- Nick Srnicek and Alex Williams, "Post-Work Imaginaries" in *Inventing the Future: Postcapitalism and a World Without Work* (London and New York: Verso, 2015), pp, 107–127. (If you can also read "Conclusion", pp. 175–183)

- J.K. Gibson-Graham, "Affects and Emotions for a Postcapitalist Politics" in *A Post-Capitalist Politics* (Minneapolis and London: University of Minnesota Press, 2006), pp. 1–22

- Paul Mason, "The Prophets of Postcapitalism" in *PostCapitalism: A Guide to Our Future* (London: Allen Lane, 2015), pp. 109–146

Lecture Two: "A Social and Psychic Revolution of Almost Inconceivable Magnitude": Countercultural Bohemia as Prefiguration

- Ellen Willis, "The Family: Love it or Leave it", in *Beginning to See the Light: Sex, Hope, and Rock-and-Roll* (Minneapolis: University of Minnesota Press, 2012), pp. 149–168

- Herbert Marcuse, "The Dialectic of Civilization" in *Eros and Civilization* (London: Abacus, 1972), pp. 68–83

Lecture Three: From Class Consciousness to Group Consciousness

- Georg Lukács, "The Standpoint of the Proletariat" from *History and Class Consciousness*. (Available online at the Marxist Internet Archive: https://www.marxists.org/archive/Lukács/works/history/)

- Nancy C. Hartsock, "The Feminist Standpoint: Developing the Ground for a Specifically Feminist Historical Materialism" in *The Feminist Standpoint Revisited and Other Essays* (Boulder, Colorado: Westview Press, 1998), pp. 105–132.

Lecture Four: "Union Power and Soul Power"

- Jefferson Cowie, "Old Fashioned Heroes of the New Working Class" in *Stayin' Alive: The 1970s and the Last Days of the Working Class* (New York and London: The New Press, 2010), pp. 23–75.

Lecture Five: Libidinal Marxism

- Jean-François Lyotard, "The Desire Named Marx" in *Libidinal Economy* (London: Athlone Press, 1993), pp. 95–149

Lecture Six: Autonomia and the Refusal of Work

- Silvia Federici, "Wages Against Housework" in *Revolution at Point Zero: Housework, Reproduction and Feminist Struggle* (Oakland: PM Press, 2012), pp. 15–21

- Nicholas Thoburn, "The Refusal of Work" in *Deleuze, Marx and Politics* (London and New York: Routledge, 2003), pp. 103–138

Lecture Seven: The Destruction of Democratic Socialism and the Origins of Neoliberalism: The Case of Chile

- Naomi Klein, "States of Shock: The Bloody Birth of

the Counterrevolution" in *The Shock Doctrine: The Rise of Disaster Capitalism* (London: Allen Lane, 2007), pp. 75–98.

- Eden Medina, "Cybernetics and Socialism" in *Cybernetic Revolutionaries: Technology and Politics in Allende's Chile* (Cambridge, Mass.: The MIT Press, 2011), pp. 15–41

Lecture Eight: The Invention of the Middle

- Carl Freedman, "Marx / Nietzsche / Freud / Nixon" in *The Age of Nixon: A Study in Cultural Power* (Winchester and Washington: Zer0 Books, 2012), pp. 71–107

- Penny Lewis, "Hardhats Versus Elite Droves: Consolidation of the Image" in *Hard Hats, Hippies and Hawks: The Vietnam Antiwar Movement as Myth and Memory* (Ithaca and London: ILR Press, 2013), pp. 159–185

Lecture Nine: Post-Fordism and New Times

- Stuart Hall, "The Meaning of New Times" in Stuart Hall and Martin Jacques (eds.), *New Times: The Changing Face of Politics in the Nineties* (London: Lawrence and Wishart, 1989), pp. 116–136

- Paolo Virno, all sections from "Beyond the Coupling of the Terms 'Fear' / 'Anguish'" through to "Intellect as Score" in *A Grammar of the Multitude: For an Analysis of Contemporary Forms of Life* (New York: Semiotext, 2004), pp. 31–66

Lecture Ten: Technofeminism / Cyberfeminism

- Shulamith Firestone, "The Two Modes of Cultural

History" in Armen Avanessian and Robin Mackay (eds.), *#ACCELERATE: The Accelerationist Reader* (Falmouth: Urbanomic, 2014), pp. 109–130

- Sadie Plant, all sections from "Cyborg Manifestos" through to "Cocoons" in *Zeros and Ones: Digital Women and the New Technoculture* (London: Fourth Estate, 1998), pp. 58–81

Lecture Eleven: Accelerationism

- Fredric Jameson, "Utopia as Replication" in *Valences of the Dialectic* (London and New York: Verso, 2009), pp. 410–435

- Nick Land, "Machinic Desire" in *Fanged Noumena: Collected Writings 1987-2007* (Falmouth: Urbanomic, 2012), pp. 319–344

Lecture Twelve: The Network and Its Discontents (1): Hardt and Negri

- Michael Hardt and Antonio Negi, "Beyond Capital?" in *Commonwealth* (Cambridge, Mass. and London: Harvard University Press, 2009), pp. 263–324

Lecture Thirteen: The Network and Its Discontents (2): Peer to Peer

- Michel Bauwens, "Peer to Peer: From Technology to Politics" in Jan Servaes and Nico Carpentier (eds.), *Towards a Sustainable Information Society: Deconstructing WSIS* (Bristol: Intellect, 2006), pp. 151–168

- Jodi Dean, "The Common and the Commons" in *The*

Communist Horizon (London and New York: Verso, 2012), pp. 119–156

Lecture Fourteen: Touchscreen Capture

- Jean Baudrillard, "The Tactile and the Digital" and "The Hyperrealism of Simulation" in *Symbolic Exchange and Death* (London, Thousand Oaks and New Delhi: SAGE, 1993), pp. 61–75

- Franco "Bifo" Berardi, "Info-Labour and 'Precarization'" in *Precarious Rhapsody* (London: Minor Compositions, 2009), pp. 30–54

Lecture Fifteen: Reinventing Prometheus

- Laboria Cuboniks, "Manifesto on Xenofeminism: A Politics for Alienation" (2015), available at http://www.laboriacuboniks.net/#zero

- Helen Hester, "Promethean Labours and Domestic Realism", available at https://www.academia.edu/11571359/Promethean_Labours_and_Domestic_Realism

Appendix Two:
"No More Miserable Monday Mornings"
Tracklist

For many of the students and staff at Goldsmiths College at the time of Fisher's death, there was no sidestepping the sense of sociopolitical impotence he had begun to describe in his lecture series. An intense desire to take up the gauntlet of radical dismantling put forth in these sessions — and in his writings more generally — was expressed almost immediately, in order to address the localised crisis of depressive anhedonia that had engulfed the university in that moment — a pervasive mental health crisis, during which Fisher's suicide was sadly not an isolated incident.

Serendipitously, it was on that first Monday morning after Fisher's death that this deeply negative moment took on a perversely affirmative resonance.

Each of the five "Postcapitalist Desire" lectures had been held first thing on a Monday morning at 9am. The sixth lecture never took place but, after news of Fisher's death on Friday the 13th spread throughout the university over the weekend, many students chose to show up in his classroom anyway on the morning of 16th January 2017.

A class of twenty doubled, perhaps trebled, in size as faces familiar and unfamiliar, from both undergraduate and postgraduate degrees, gathered together on an abjectly miserable Monday morning, waiting for Fisher himself to walk through the door and reveal his hoax.

After some time spent in silence, an impromptu listening session began instead.

Although it was likely just an arbitrary instance of administrative scheduling, it was hard not to imbue the timing of Fisher's lectures with some deeper significance. The penultimate post on his famous *k-punk* blog, before it fell silent forever, had presented an audio mix, fittingly entitled: "No more miserable Monday mornings" — a title that would also find itself repurposed within his unfinished *Acid Communism* introduction. It was a phrase that recast that old anti-capitalist adage in a newly positive light: "You don't hate Mondays, you hate your job". In the immediate context of Fisher's life, it took on a double meaning, as both a call for the end of work and perhaps a sly Lyotardian acknowledgment that he nonetheless loved working with his students, who likewise loved working with him. With this understanding in mind, it was this mix that Fisher's students chose to listen to on that mournful Monday morning in mid-January.

The mix starts, appropriately, with Sleaford Mods' "Jobseeker" before passing through the rise and fall of the counterculture. Psychedelic pop gives way to dub which gives way to disco. The pressure cooker of twenty-first-century working-class fury finds itself harnessed and redirected until the mix fades out to Chic's blissful 1978 track "At Last I Am Free".

The mix is a tonic, and a mode of consciousness-raising presented chronologically in reverse, where the political fury of today re-establishes contact with the collective joy of the counterculture. But this mix is not a nostalgic longing for a lost moment. It simply takes advantage of the fact that these songs, these cultural artefacts, still exist and are still at our disposal — much like the potentials they represent.

In this sense, it is a mix that emphasises the political

function of each track over its aesthetic form. Taken as a whole, it auto-affects the brain into a state of joyful indignation reigniting an aesthetic moment long since reified into an all too timely collection of commodified genres and fetishised vinyl records. Despite this process of aesthetic reification, the freedoms these songs promise remain soulful, and this emboldened soul rattles the subjugated body out of its contemporary complacency. It is a mix that may slide from 2008 to 1978, but the message nonetheless remains future-oriented. There are alternatives and there are tomorrows. There is a world to be transformed.

***

1.	"Jobseeker" by Sleaford Mods
	(*The Mekon*, 2008)

2.	"House in the Country" by The Kinks
	(*Face to Face*, 1966)

3.	"Rat Race" by The Specials
	(*The Specials*, 1979)

4.	"Too Much Work Load" by Singers & Players
	(*Revenge of the Underdog*, 1982)

5.	"Boss Man" by Rhythm & Sound
	(*See Mi Yah*, 2005)

6.	"Tethered to my Hot-Spot" by eMMplekz
	(*Your Crate Has Changed*, 2013)

7.	"Smithers-Jones" by The Jam
	(*Setting Sons*, 1979)

8. "I'm Gonna Tear Your Playhouse Down"
by Ann Peebles (*I Can't Stand the Rain*, 1974)

9. "Spaceship" by Kanye West feat. GLC and
Consequence (*The College Dropout*, 2004)

10. "Chant No. 1 (I Don't Need This Pressure
On)" by Spandau Ballet (*Diamond*, 1982)

11. "Stoned Love" by The Supremes
(*New Ways but Love Stays*, 1970)

12. "Psychedelic Shack" by The Temptations
(*Psychedelic Shack*, 1970)

13. "Off the Wall" by Michael Jackson
(*Off the Wall*, 1979)

14. "Can't Stop Playing (Makes Me High)"
by Dr Kucho! & Gregor Salt (2015)

15. "Lost in Music (Special 1984 Nile Rogers
Remix)" by Sister Sledge (1984)

16. "At Last I Am Free" by Chic
(*C'est Chic*, 1978)

From anger and sadness to collective joy ... from work
that never ends to endless free time ...

Universal Basic Income now!

k-punk, 18 July 2015[1]

Notes

INTRODUCTION: NO MORE MISERABLE MONDAY MORNINGS

1   Mark Fisher, "k-punk, or the glampunk art pop discontinuum" in *k-punk: The Collected and Unpublished Writings of Mark Fisher (2004-2016)*, ed. Darren Ambrose. London: Repeater Books, 2018, 273.

2   Ibid., 275.

3   Mark Fisher, "Megalithic Astropunk", *Hyperstition* blog, 6 February 2005: ‹http://hyperstition.abstractdynamics.org/archives/004932.html›

4   Mark Fisher, "Why Burroughs is a Cold Rationalist", *k-punk* blog, 29 August 2004: ‹http://k-punk.abstractdynamics.org/archives/004035.html›

5   Mark Fisher, "Psychedelic Reason", *k-punk* blog, 19 August 2004: ‹http://k-punk.abstractdynamics.org/archives/003926.html›

6   Mark Fisher, "Emotional Engineering", *k-punk* blog, 3 August 2004: ‹http://k-punk.abstractdynamics.org/archives/003767.html›

7   Ibid.

8   Ibid.

9   Fisher, "Psychedelic Reason".

10 Ibid.

11 Ibid.

12 Fisher, "k-punk, or the glampunk art pop discontinuum", 275.

13 Ibid., 275–276.

14 Consider, for instance, the strange fate of the Beatles' 1967

album, *Sgt. Pepper's Lonely Hearts Club Band*. Whilst many continue to view this maximalist studio explosion as a revolutionary moment for pop, its legacy has waned in the minds of many a more politically-conscious critic, for whom its effervescence died with the counterculture. Others have argued it was made almost immediately redundant by the socio-political upheavals in Europe the following year, in May 1968.

15   Mark Fisher, "Acid Communism (Unfinished Introduction)", *k-punk*, 759.

16   Mark Fisher, "Portmeirion: An Ideal for Living", *k-punk*, 120.

17   Ibid., 770.

18   Ibid.

19   Reza Negarestani, *Cyclonopedia: Complicity with Anonymous Materials*. Victoria: re.press, 2008.

20   Mark Fisher, "Postcapitalist Desire" in *What Are We Fighting For: A Radical Collective Manifesto*, eds. Federico Campagna and Emanuele Campiglio. London: Pluto Books, eBook, 2012, 328–329.

21   Ibid., 330.

22   Ibid.

23   Nick Land, "Machinic Desire" in *Fanged Noumena: Collected Writings 1987-2007*. Falmouth and New York: Urbanomic; Sequences Press, 2011, 339.

24   Ibid., 343.

25   Mark Fisher, "'A social and psychic revolution of almost inconceivable magnitude': Popular Culture's Interrupted Accelerationist Dreams", *e-flux*, June 2013: <https://www.e-flux.com/journal/46/60084/a-social-and-psychic-revolution-of-almost-inconceivable-magnitude-popular-culture-s-interrupted-accelerationist-dreams/>

26   Mark Fisher, "Exiting the Vampire Castle", *k-punk*, 738–739.

27   Mark Fisher, "Mommy, What's a Grey Vampire?", *k-punk* blog, 21 June 2009: <http://k-punk.abstractdynamics.org/archives/011192.html>

28   Fisher, "Exiting the Vampire Castle", 739.

29 Fisher, "No Romance Without Finance", *k-punk*, 421.

30 See: Mark Fisher, *Capitalist Realism: Is There No Alternative?* London: Zer0 Books, 2009, 66: "The required subject — a collective subject — does not exist, yet the crisis, like all the other global crises we're now facing, demands that it be constructed".

31 Fisher, "No Romance Without Finance", 420.

32 Fisher, "Classless broadcasting: Benefits Street", *k-punk*, 237.

33 The moralising tendencies demonstrated by the likes of *Benefits Street* have seemingly fallen out of favour in more recent years. However, the bourgeois gaze remains the default, even in many television programmes that proclaim to embody a far more progressive attitude to the genre of reality television. For example, the 2018 reboot of the mid-2000s make-over show, *Queer Eye for the Straight Guy* — now simply *Queer Eye* — prides itself on its willingness to challenge social norms, but class is almost entirely absent from any of the show's conversations, as the so-called "Fab 5" portray well-being and self-care to be the new forms of etiquette epitomised by middle-class tastes and behaviours.

34 Jean-François Lyotard, *Libidinal Economy*, trans. Iain Hamilton Grant. London and New York: Bloomsbury Academic, 2015, 128.

35 Ibid., 123-124.

36 Mark Fisher, "Terminator Versus Avatar" in *#ACCELERATE: The Accelerationist Reader*, eds. Robin Mackay and Armen Avanessian. Falmouth and Berlin: Urbanomic; Merve, 2014, 339.

37 Ibid., 340.

38 Sleaford Mods, "Jobseeker", *The Mekon* (A52 Sounds, 2008); *Chubbed Up: The Singles Collection* (Ipecac Recordings, 2014).

39 Mark Fisher, "Review: Sleaford Mods' *Divide and Exit* and *Chubbed Up*", *k-punk*, 413.

40 Ibid.

41 Ibid.

42 Pete Wolfendale, "So, Accelerationism, What's All That Above?", *Deontologistics* blog, 18 February 2018: <https://deontologistics.wordpress.com/2018/02/18/ofta-so-accelerationism-whats-all-that-about/>

43 See: Benjamin Noys, *The Persistence of the Negative: A Critique of Contemporary Continental Theory*. Edinburgh: Edinburgh University Press, 2012.

44 This crisis of the negative can be attributed to the philosopher Alain Badiou who, in a 2007 interview, argued: "Contrary to Hegel, for whom the negation of the negation produces a new affirmation, I think we must assert that today negativity, properly speaking, does not create anything new. It destroys the old, of course, but does not give rise to a new creation." From this moment, we can see Fisher's writings on accelerationism and hauntology not as distinct interests but as entwined interests. Whereas hauntology explores this crisis, accelerationism seeks to correct it. See: Alain Badiou, Jason Smith and Filippo del Luchesse, "'We Need a Popular Discipline': Contemporary Politics and the Crisis of the Negative — Interview with Alain Badiou", *Lacanian Ink*, 7 February 2007: <https://www.lacan.com/baddiscipline.html>

45 For more on the innately productive nature of Fisher's hauntology, see: Matt Colquhoun, "Music Has The Right To Children: Reframing Mark Fisher's Hauntology", *The Quietus*, 15 March 2020: <https://thequietus.com/articles/27968-matt-colquhoun-egress-mark-fisher-hauntology-essay>

46 Noys, *The Persistence of the Negative*, 5.

47 Wolfendale, "So, Accelerationism, What's All That About?"

48 Georg Lukács, *History & Class Consciousness: Studies in Marxist Dialectics*, trans. Rodney Livingstone. Cambridge, Mass.: The MIT Press, 1971, 197.

49 Ibid., 143.

50 Deleuze and Guattari famously consider the peculiarities of this view of history and what it has done to our under-

standing of the modern subject and its values. See: Gilles Deleuze and Félix Guattari, "10,000 B.C.: The Geology of Morals (Who Does the Earth Think It Is?)" in *A Thousand Plateaus*. London: Bloomsbury Academic, 2013.

51   Lukács, *History & Class Consciousness*, 144.

52   Ibid., 186.

53   Ibid.

54   Wolfendale, "So, Accelerationism, What's All That About?"

55   Ibid.

56   Ibid.

57   Nicholas Thoburn, *Deleuze, Marx and Politics*. London: Routledge, 2003, 1.

58   Ibid.

59   For more on "Acid Corbynism", see: Casper Hughes, "Why Acid Corbynism is the new counterculture we need", *The Independent*, 28 February 2018: <https://www.independent.co.uk/voices/acid-corbynism-labour-jeremy-corbyn-counter-culture-a8231936.html>

LECTURE ONE: WHAT IS POSTCAPITALISM?

1   Apple's 1984 Super Bowl commercial is available to watch here via YouTube: <https://youtu.be/2zfqw8nhUwA>

2   Given how heavily the advert drew on the imagery of *1984*, the George Orwell estate deemed the advert to be an infringement of their copyright and sent a cease-and-desist letter to Apple. See: William R. Coulson, "'Big Brother' is Watching Apple: The Truth About the Super Bowl's Most Famous Ad". *Dartmouth Law Journal*. Winter 2009, 7 (1): 106–115.

3   A term coined during Fisher's time with the Cybernetic Culture Research Unit at the University of Warwick in the late 1990s, "hyperstition", in its most rudimentary form, refers to a process whereby fictions make themselves real. The Ccru define it for themselves as follows: "Element of

effective culture that makes itself real, through fictional quantities functioning as time-travelling potentials. Hyperstition operates as a coincidence intensifier, effecting a call to the Old Ones." See: Ccru, "Appendix 1: Ccru Glossary", *Ccru Writings 1997-2003*. Falmouth: Urbanomic Media, 2017, 363.

4   The VLE refers to the university's "Virtual Learning Environment" — an institutional server for sharing educational materials, departmental news, and other information amongst the staff and student bodies.

5   "Levi's 1984 Russia" is available to view on YouTube here: <https://www.youtube.com/watch?v=Z3pe-3ZnL8Y>

6   This clip from *Have I Got News for You* is available to watch on YouTube here: <https://www.youtube.com/watch?v=3252FSW7OC4>

7   "May '68" refers to a period of civil unrest in France, when leftist student protests joined forces with a workers' general strike. The unrest, which centred around universities and factories, brought the country's economy to a standstill and very nearly brought down the French government.

8   Only Antonio Negri was involved in Autonomia. Michael Hardt, born in 1960, and twenty-five years Negri's junior, was in America and in his mid-teens when the movement began.

9   "Touchscreen Capture" is another seminar topic which takes its name directly from one of Fisher's previous essays. See: Mark Fisher, "Touchscreen Capture", *noon: An Annual Journal of Visual Culture and Contemporary Art*, Vol. 6: Post-Online. Gwangju, South Korea: Gwangju Biennale Foundation, 2016.

10   Text from slide 5:

What are some of the advantages of the concept of postcapitalism (over communism, socialism etc.)?

   1.   *It is not tainted by association with past failed and oppressive projects.*

   2.   *It implies victory – capitalism will end and be replaced by something else.*

3.   It starts from what and where we are – what capitalism has already built – its pleasures as well as its oppressions.

11   Text from slide 6:

What are some of the disadvantages of the concept of postcapitalism?

1.   It remains tied to capitalism (i.e. it might be guilty of 'capitalocentrism').

2.   It does not name a positive project.

3.   It remains in the temporality of the 'post-'.

4.   Not necessarily progressive (see Peter Frase's Four Futures: Life After Capitalism — only two of the four futures are progressive!)

12   See: Peter Frase, *Four Futures: Life After Capitalism*. London: Verso Books, 2016.

13   "Luxury Communism" is a term that has its roots in the mid-2000s protest movements that followed the financial crash. See: Brian Merchant, "Fully automated luxury communism", *The Guardian*, 18 March 2015: <https://www. theguardian.com/sustainable-business/2015/mar/18/ fully-automated-luxury-communism-robots-employment>. See also: Aaron Bastani, *Fully Automated Luxury Communism*. London: Verso Books, 2019.

14   Images from slides 7 and 8 were sourced from: "Mapping the Emerging Post-Capitalist Paradigm and its Main Thinkers", *Commons Transition*, 2 December 2015: <http://common-stransition.org/mapping-the-emerging-post-capitalist-para-digm-and-its-main-thinkers/>

15   J.K. Gibson-Graham, *A Post-Capitalist Politics*. Minneapolis and London: University of Minnesota Press, 2006, 4. [Slide 9].

16   Ibid., 5. [Slide 10].

17   Wendy Brown, "Wounded Attachments", *Political Theory*, Vol. 21, No. 3 (Aug., 1993), 390–410.

18   Gibson-Graham, *A Post-Capitalist Politics*, 5–6. [Slide 11].

19   See: Walter Benjamin, "Left-Wing Melancholy", *The Weimar Republic Sourcebook*, eds. A. Kaes, M. Jay, and E. Dimendberg.

Berkeley: University of California Press, 1994.

20   Gibson-Graham, *A Post-Capitalist Politics*, 6. [Slide 12].

21   Text from slide 13:

Gibson-Graham on the impasses of 'modernist class politics'

> *'On one level, the crisis of modernist class politics is a crisis of desire, and where the two films diverge most is in the representation of that crisis. In* Brassed Off, *desire is stuck: on keeping the mines open; on being employed (and thus exploited by capital); on solidarity based on shared male experience, including that of capitalist exploitation; on keeping alive communities built on exploitation as well as life-destroying work. Desire is stalemated in a fixation on the demand of the capitalist Other — for labor and for an antagonistic political complement, the "working class".'*

Taken from Gibson-Graham, *A Post-Capitalist Politics*, 11.

22   Text from slide 14:

How to overcome these impasses?

> **Dislocation – moving beyond 'capitalocentrism'.** *'We can begin to "unfix" economic identity by deconstructing the dominant capitalocentric discourse of economy in which capitalist economic activity is taken as the model for all economic activity. We can dislocate the unity and hegemony of neoliberal global capitalist economic discourse through a proliferative queering of the economic landscape and construction of a new language of economic diversity. This dislocation is a crucial prerequisite to the project of cultivating different subjects of economy.'*

23   Gibson-Graham, *A Post-Capitalist Politics*, 56.

24   Image from Slide 15: Figure 18 from Gibson-Graham, *A Post-Capitalist Politics*, 70: "The iceberg. From *Community Economies Collective* 2001; drawn by Ken Byrne".

25   Gibson-Graham, *A Post-Capitalist Politics*, 56.

26   Text from slide 16:

G-G on the importance of feminism for moving beyond the traditional party

> **Alternative organisational forms:** *"organizational horizontalism" fostered alternative ways of being (powerful), including*

'direct and equitable participation, non-monopoly of the spoken word or of information, the rotation of occasional tasks and responsibilities, the non-specialization of functions, the non-delegation of power' (Alvarez, Dagnino, and Escobar 1998, 97)

'the loosely interrelated struggles and happenings of the feminist movement were capable of mobilizing social transformation at such an unprecedented scale, without resort to a vanguard party or any of the other "necessities" we have come to associate with political organization. The complex intermixing of alternative discourses, shared language, embodied practices, self-cultivation, emplaced actions, and global transformation associated with second-wave feminism has nourished our thinking about a politics of economic possibility — impressing us with the strikingly simple ontological contours of a feminist imaginary: if women are everywhere, a woman is always somewhere, and those places of women are transformed as women transform themselves.'

27   Gibson-Graham, *A Post-Capitalist Politics*, 56.

28   Ibid., xxiv.

29   Text from slide 17:

G-G on moving beyond the affects associated with traditional left politics

New affects: 'The affects associated with this becoming community are not those traditionally linked to left politics — the outrage and anger that cluster around heroic struggles, or the cynicism and righteousness that operate in left political movements as a powerful emotional undertow. Affect in the film has an enticing quality of wonder as awareness of and delight in otherness take hold of the characters. In this utopian atmosphere, distrust, misrecognition, and judgment are temporarily suspended and a solidarity develops that is based not on sameness, but on a growing recognition that the other is what makes self possible — climaxing in the moment when audience and performers come together and make possible both the performance and each other's roles within it.'.

30   Gibson-Graham, *A Post-Capitalist Politics*, 18.

31   Ibid.

32   *Ressentiment* is a term most often associated with the work
      of Friedrich Nietzsche, used to describe a kind of reactionary
      hostility towards anything outside of one's self, particu-
      larly when regarding one's social position. It is part of his
      problematising of Hegel's famous 'master-slave' dialectic and
      names a kind of inferiority complex defined by an impotent
      fury that is more self-flagellating than actively revolutionary.
      As Nietzsche writes: "The beginning of the slaves' revolt in
      morality occurs when *ressentiment* itself turns creative and
      gives birth to values: the *ressentiment* of those beings who,
      denied the proper response of action, compensate for it only
      with imaginary revenge. Whereas all noble morality grows
      out of a triumphant saying 'yes' to itself, slave morality
      says 'no' on principle to everything that is 'outside', 'other',
      'non-self': and *this* 'no' is its creative deed. This reversal of
      the evaluating glance — this *essential* orientation to the
      outside instead of back onto itself — is a feature of *ressen-
      timent*: in order to come about, slave morality first has to
      have an opposing, external world, it needs, physiologically
      speaking, external stimuli in order to act at all, — its action
      is basically a reaction." See: Friedrich Nietzsche, *On the
      Genealogy of Morality*, ed. Keith Ansell-Pearson, trans. Carol
      Diethe. Cambridge: Cambridge University Press, Revised
      Student edition, 2007, 20.

33   Text from slide 18:

The community economy versus the mainstream/ capitalist economy
   *Lakshman Yapa (2014) Take Back the Economy: An Ethical Guide
   for Transforming Our Communities, The AAG Review of Books,
   2:1, 25-29 [Hyperlink: <http://www.tandfonline.com/doi/
   pdf/10.1080/2325548X.2014.894422>]*
   *'To Gibson-Graham, Cameron ...., taking back the economy
   through ethical action means the following:*
   •   *Surviving together well and equitably.*

- *Distributing surplus to enrich social and environmental health.*
- *Encountering others in ways that support their well-being as well as ours.*
- *Consuming sustainably.*
- *Caring for—maintaining, replenishing, and growing—our natural and cultural commons.*
- *Investing our wealth in future generations so that they can live as well. Following this the authors aver:*

  > *"An Economy centered on these ethical considerations is what we call a community economy—a space of decision making where we recognize and negotiate our inter-dependence with other humans, other species, and our environment. In the process of recognizing and negoti-ating, we become a community".' (p. xix)*

34   Gibson-Graham, *A Post-Capitalist Politics*, xix.

35   Image from slide 19: Figure 23 from Gibson-Graham, *A Post-Capitalist Politics*, 80: "Key words of economy and community economy. From Bernard and Young (1997), Crouch and Marquand (1995), Meeker-Lowry (1995), Ife (1995), Pearce (1993), Power (1996), and Wildman (1993)".

36   Nick Srnicek and Alex Williams, "#Accelerate: Manifesto for an Accelerationist Politics" in *#ACCELERATE: The Accelera-tionist Reader*, eds. Robin Mackay and Armen Avanessian. Falmouth and Berlin: Urbanomic; Merve, 2014, 354. [Slide 20].

37   Text from slide 21:
Srnicek and Williams on demands for a post-work society
This entails:
(first of all) the demand for demands themselves ('A politics with demands is simply a collection of aimless bodies')
These demands should take the form of non-reformist reforms. These reforms (1) have a utopian/ antagonistic component and (2) are based in actual tendencies at work in the world today

38   Nick Srnicek and Alex Williams, *Inventing the Future: Postcap-*

italism and a World Without Work. London and New York: Verso, 2015, 107.

39   Ibid., 108.

40   Ibid.

41   Ibid., 109. [Slide 22].

42   Text read aloud from slide 23.

43   Text from slide 24:
     The demand for a reduced working week

·   *A return to one of the classic demands of the workers' movement*

·   *It is a positive response to rising automation*

·   *It has environmental advantages (reduced commuting and work-related consumption)*

·   *It increases the power of workers – would require action from trade unions and other groups (i.e. associations of precarious workers)*

44   Text from slide 25:
     The demand for a universal basic income
     It must be sufficient and universal – a supplement to existing welfare arrangements not a substitute for them
     Four key arguments:

     1.   *A political transformation – the proletariat can subsist with a job – producing an increase in class power.*
     2.   *Precarity is transformed into flexibility on workers' terms.*
     3.   *Changes how work is valued — boring, repetitive, and dangerous work would be highly paid; creative and intrinsically rewarding work would be less well paid.*
     4.   *A feminist proposal – allows experimentation with the family structure.*

45   Text from slide 26: *The demand for a diminishment of the work ethic*
     Reversing the link between suffering and remuneration.
     A counter-hegemonic approach – which can draw upon already-existing hatred of jobs!

46   *Benefits Street* was actually broadcast on Channel 4 in the UK. This was partly why the programme was so outrageous, as

the channel had previously been renowned for its progressive programming in the 1980s and 1990s. Unfortunately, as Fisher noted in his 2014 essay on the programme for *New Humanist*, *Benefits Street* was then "part of a disingenuous trend in documentary making. Writing [in 2013] for the journal the *Sociological Imagination*, Tracy Jensen predicted a 'summer of poverty porn', citing such programmes as *How To Get A Council House*, *Why Don't You Speak English?*, *Benefits Britain 1949* (all Channel 4) and *We All Pay Your Benefits* (BBC1)." He writes later: "It's a mark of how bad Channel 4's programming now is that *Benefits Street* would probably count as one of its serious recent attempts at documentary. If you want to measure the catastrophic impact of neoliberalism on British culture, then there's no better example than Channel 4. A channel that began with programming that included European art films, serious philosophy discussion programmes and politically sophisticated documentaries has now degenerated into depths so embarrassingly hucksterish and craven that they are beyond parody." See: Mark Fisher, "Classless Broadcasting: *Benefits Street*", *k-punk*, 236 and 238.

47   Text from slide 27:
Mason's version of postcapitalism
Based on the theory of Kondratiev waves – the idea that capitalism renews itself in 'long waves of growth' – but there is no sign of renewal – capitalism is stuck in a long downswing
Partly this is because of its own triumph – i.e. neoliberalism's success in subduing the working class has removed capital's main driver of renewal (struggle against the working class forced capital to innovate)

48   Text from slide 28:
Precursor: Drucker on the centrality of knowledge
- *Peter Drucker – Post-Capitalist Society*
- *Key claim: knowledge has become the key resource in contemporary society*
- *Key questions: how can we improve the productivity of*

knowledge?

- *Who is the social archetype of the new society? 'The universal educated person' – according to Mason this person has arrived in the form of the 'networked individual'*

49   Text from slide 29:

'Info-goods change everything'

'Once the cost of creating a new set of instructions has been incurred, the instructions can be used over and over again at no additional cost.' (Romer)

Info-capitalism responds by making it illegal to copy certain kinds of data – 'With info-capitalism, a monopoly … is the only way an industry can run.'

It breaks the basic law of economics: that everything is scarce

Info-goods operate via 'non-rivalry' (just because I have one does not stop you having one – in fact value is added via sharing)

Open Source versus Microsoft

50   Text from slide 30:

The case of Wikipedia

Could Wikipedia have been created by capitalist dynamics alone? Is Open-source or ('commons-based peer to peer production') the model for a new set of social and economic relations? (Mason: 'At the precise moment in history when it became possible to produce stuff without the market or the firm, significant numbers of people started doing so')

This is part of 'a new sustainable mode of production' (Benkler)

'If a free-market economy with intellectual property leads to the underutilization of information, then an economy based on the full utilization of information cannot have a free market or absolute property rights'.

51   Text from slide 31:

The General Intellect

In The Fragment on Machines, *Marx envisages a world in which the worker steps to the side of the production process – becoming a supervisor rather than an operator of machines – the productive power of the cotton-spinning machine, the telegraph and the steam locomotive was out of proportion to the labour time spent on their production but depended on science and technology.*

In a world dominated by such machines, knowledge must be social.

Capital will be forced to develop the knowledge of the worker – technology develops as part of a 'General Intellect'

52 Paul Mason, *Postcapitalism: A Guide to Our Future*. London: Allen Lane, 2015, 144. [Slide 32].

53 See: David Graeber, "On the Phenomenon of Bullshit Jobs", *STRIKE! Magazine*. Issue 3, "The Summer of...", August 2013: <https://www.strike.coop/bullshit-jobs/> This essay was later adapted into a book. See also: David Graeber, *Bullshit Jobs: A Theory*. London: Allen Lane, 2018.

54 Mason, *Postcapitalism*, 144. [Slide 32].

55 Ben Schiller, "Welcome to the Post-Work Economy", *Fast Company*, 15 March 2016: <https://www.fastcompany.com/3056483/welcome-to-the-post-work-economy>

56 Text from Slide 33:

Mason's five principles of transition

1. *Understand the limits of human will-power*
2. *Ecological sustainability*
3. *The transition must be a human as well as an economic transition*
4. *Attack the problem from all angles*
5. *Maximise the power of information*

57 Text from slide 34:

Steps towards this transition

1. *An accurate and open-source computer simulation of current economic reality*
2. *A shift to a 'wiki-state' model, which would: switch off the privatization models; reshape markets towards 'sustainable, collaborative and socially just outcomes'; make space for collaborative, P2P and non-profit activities; force corporations to drive change*
3. *Suppress or socialize monopolies*

4. Let market forces disappear – some markets can survive (with limited patents and intellectual property) but market forces must be suppressed entirely in wholesale energy
5. Socialise the finance system
6. Pay everyone a basic income
7. Unleash the network!

LECTURE TWO: "A SOCIAL AND PSYCHIC REVOLUTION OF ALMOST INCONCEIVABLE MAGNITUDE": COUNTER-CULTURAL BOHEMIA AS PREFIGURATION

1   Sigmund Freud, "Totem and Taboo" in *The Origins of Religion*, trans. James Strachey, ed. Albert Dickson. London: Penguin Books; The Pelican Freud Library, Vol. 13, 185.
2   Ibid., 186.
3   Freud's *Totem and Taboo* was originally published in 1913.
4   This is in reference to University College London, which has in its possession the severed and badly-preserved head of English philosopher Jeremy Bentham (1748–1832).
5   It is Jacques Lacan who makes this pun, writing on the "nom du père" and the "non du père". See: Jacques Lacan, *The Seminar of Jacques Lacan Book Three: The Psychoses*. New York: W. W. Norton & Company, 1997. Foucault has also commented on this pun within Lacan's work. See: Michel Foucault, "The Father's No" in *Aesthetics, Method and Epistemology: Essential Works of Foucault, 1954-1984 (Volume Two)*. New York: The New Press, 1998, 5–20.
6   "Sex, Gender, Species" was a separate postgraduate module that could also be chosen as part of the MA in Contemporary Art Theory, run by Dr Lynn Turner.
7   Herbert Marcuse, *Eros and Civilization*. London: Abacus, 1972, 70.
8   Sigmund Freud, "'Civilised' Sexual Morality and Modern Nervousness", in *Collected Papers*. (London: Hogarth press, 1950), II, 82.

9   Marcuse, *Eros and Civilization*, 70.

10   Ibid.

11   Ibid., 72.

12   Ibid., 75.

13   Ibid., 76–77.

14   Ibid., 80.

15   Ibid.

16   Marcuse refers to the "performance principle" as "the prevailing historical form of the *reality principle*" (Ibid., 35) — Freud's term for the drive central to the ego, which negotiates and sees the world through the tension produced by superego and id, i.e. counter to the "pleasure principle". Whereas Freud would later write *Beyond the Pleasure Principle*, we might argue that Marcuse's text is his *Beyond the Reality Principle*. This position foreshadows Fisher's Spinozist psychedelic reason. For Marcuse, "beyond the performance principle, the gratification of the instinct requires the more conscious effort of free rationality, the less it is the by-product of the superimposed rationality of oppression." (Ibid., 223.)

17   Ibid., 83.

18   Ellen Willis, *Beginning to See the Light: Sex, Hope, and Rock-and-Roll*. Minneapolis: University of Minnesota Press, 2012, 158.

19   This question has been reignited in more recent years. See: Sophie Lewis, *Full Surrogacy Now: Feminism Against Family*. London: Verso Books, 2019.

20   The emancipation of women is referenced frequently throughout Srnicek and Williams' text, *Inventing the Future*. More specifically, Fisher is here referring to an argument made regarding the abolition of work and the move towards the full automation of society. Srnicek and Williams argue at one point, for instance, that archaic attitudes towards what is stereotypically thought of as "women's work" remains detrimental to how we consider such issues. "Indeed, the stereotype that women are naturally nurturing and desiring

of this affective labour is often a pernicious cover for their continued exploitation. But what if much of this labour could be eliminated? ... [I]ncreasingly, domestic tasks like cleaning the house and folding clothes, for example, can be delegated to machines. ... More speculatively, some have argued that the pain and suffering involved in pregnancy is something that should be relegated to the past, rather than mystified as natural and beautiful. In this vision, synthetic forms of biological reproduction would enable a newfound equality between the sexes." (*Inventing the Future*, 113.) This has explicit implications for the establishment of a Universal Basic Income. They continue: "a basic income would not only transform the value of the worst jobs, but also go some way towards recognising the unpaid labour of most care work. In the same way that the demand for wages for housework recognised and politicised the domestic labour of women, so too does UBI recognise and politicise the generalised way in which we are all responsible for reproducing society: from informal to formal work, from domestic to public work, from individual to collective work." (Ibid., 122.)

21 'Big Flame' was a working-class political group comprised of socialists, libertarian Marxists, Trotskyists and anarchists, that emerged from the factories in and around Liverpool in the UK in 1970 and operated around the UK up until their dissolution in 1984. The group published a magazine and a more theoretical journal and were hugely influential amongst British Marxists of the time.

22 A reference to Deleuze and Guattari's *Anti-Oedipus*, the second chapter of which begins: "Oedipus restrained is the figure of the daddy-mommy-me triangle, the familial constellation in person." See: Gilles Deleuze and Félix Guattari, *Anti-Oedipus*, trans. Robert Hurley and Mark Seem. London and New York: Bloomsbury Academic, 2004, 67.

23 *All Watched Over by Machines of Loving Grace* was a three-part documentary series by filmmaker Adam Curis, first broadcast

on the BBC in 2011.

24 In his first major work, *The Divided Self* (1960), Laing describes the emergence in psychoanalysis of the concept of the "schizophrenogenic" mother. This mother is (inadvertently) responsible for the conflicting notions of self that leads to schizophrenic tendencies in their children. Laing, however, extends this notion. He writes: "Not only the mother but also the total family situation may impede rather than facilitate the child's capacity to participate in a real shared world, as self-with-other." (See: R.D. Laing, *The Divided Self: An Existential Study in Sanity and Madness*. London: Penguin Books, 2010, 189.) This notion would later come to dominate Laing's writings, particularly in his later works *Sanity, Madness and the Family (1964)* and *The Politics of the Family and Other Essays* (1971). David Cooper was writing around a similar time. His central work on the family, *The Death of the Family*, was also published in 1971. Notably, Cooper had previously edited *Dialectics of Liberation*, a volume collecting papers delivered at The Congress of the Dialectics of Liberation in London in 1967, including presentations by Gregory Bateson, whose conception of schizophrenia would be a central influence on Deleuze and Guattari, and also Herbert Marcuse.

25 In his 1943 paper "A Theory of Human Motivation", Abraham Maslow put forward the theory that human needs — human desires, effectively — could be structured hierarchically. The foundational needs, our "basic needs", were at the base — food, water, sleep, shelter, security — followed by our psychological needs — friends, family, relationships in general, self-esteem — with needs of self-fulfilment at the top — the need to be creative, to progress, to achieve our potential. This theory was, and arguably remains, hugely influential in some fields when it comes to thinking about the motivations behind various human behaviours.

26 Willis, *Beginning to See the Light*, 161.

27   This is a reference to Donald Trump's election to the American presidency in November 2016.

28   See: Luc Boltanski and Eve Chiapello, *The New Spirit of Capitalism*, trans. Gregory Elliott. London: Verso, 2017.

29   Apple's 1984 Super Bowl commercial, discussed in Lecture 1.

LECTURE THREE: FROM CLASS CONSCIOUSNESS TO GROUP CONSCIOUSNESS

1   See: David Graeber, *The Utopia of Rules: On Technology, Stupidity and the Secret Joys of Bureaucracy*. New York and London: Melville House, 2015.

2   This is a reference to a quite humorous passage from *Analysis of the Phenomena of the Human Mind*, a 1829 work by Scottish historian and empiricist James Mill. Explaining his theory of synchronous sensations, he writes: "Among the objects which I have thus observed synchronically, or successively; that is, from which I have had synchronical or successive sensations; there are some which I have so observed frequently; others which I have so observed not frequently: in other words, of my sensations some have been frequently synchronical, others not frequently; some frequently successive, others not frequently. Thus, my sight of roast beef, and my taste of roast beef has been frequently synchronical..." See: James Mill, *Analysis of the Phenomena of the Human Mind, Volume 1*. London: Longmans Green Reader and Dyer, 1869, 73-77.

3   Here Mark is referring to former British prime minister Margaret Thatcher's comment in an interview with *Women's Own* magazine in 1987, in which she declared, when asked about an apparent fall in social cohesion, "there's no such thing as society. There are individual men and women and there are families. And no government can do anything except through people, and people must look after themselves first. It is our duty to look after ourselves and then, also, to look after our neighbours".

4   See: Fredric Jameson, "Cognitive Mapping" in Nelson, Cary, and Lawrence Grossberg (eds.), *Marxism and the Interpretation of Culture*. Urbana and Chicago: University of Illinois Press, 1988.

5   See: Nancy Hartsock, *The Feminist Standpoint Revisited and Other Essays*. Boulder, Colorado: Westview Press, 1998, 114: "Thus, the male worker in the process of production, is involved in contact with necessity, and interchange with nature as well as with other human beings but the process of production or work does not consume his whole life. The activity of a woman in the home as well as the work she does for wages keeps her continually in contact with a world of qualities and change. Her immersion in the world of use — in concrete, many-qualitied, changing material processes — is more complete than his. And if life itself consists of sensuous activity, the vantage point available to women on the basis of their contribution to subsistence represents an intensification and deepening of the materialist world view and consciousness available to the producers of commodities in capitalism, an intensification of class consciousness. The availability of this outlook to even non-working-class women has been strikingly formulated by Marilyn French in *The Women's Room*: 'Washing the toilet used by three males, and the floor and walls around it, is, Mira thought, coming face to face with necessity. And that is why women were saner than men, did not come up with the mad, absurd schemes men developed; they were in touch with necessity, they had to wash the toilet bowl and floor.'"

6   See: Charles Dickens, *Great Expectations*. London: Penguin Books, 1996, 60. As Pip and Estella play a game of cards, she comments on his appearance and his apparently unusual name for the Jacks in a pack of cards: "'He calls the knaves, Jacks, this boy!' said Estella with disdain, before our first game was out. 'And what coarse hands he has! And what thick boots!' I had never thought of being ashamed of my hands before; but I began to consider them a very indifferent pair.

Her contempt for me was so strong, that it became infectious, and I caught it".

7   "Too much cheesecake too soon / Old money's better than new / No mention in the latest Tribune / And don't let this happen to you". "Editions of You" by Roxy Music, from *For Your Pleasure* (Island Records, 1973).

8   The twelfth lecture of the "Postcapitalist Desire" course — "The Network and its Discontents (1)" — was scheduled to consider Hardt and Negri's 2009 text *Commonwealth*.

9   See: Gary Younge, "How Trump Took Middle America", *The Guardian*, 16 November 2016: <https://www.theguardian.com/membership/2016/nov/16/how-trump-took-middletown-muncie-election> "The connection between closed factories and the rise of the populist right is threefold. First, people are desperate. They were desperate before the economic crisis. It's not that there are no jobs available in Muncie. As well as the university and hospital, some new manufacturing jobs have arrived. But none can provide the kind of lifestyle to which previous generations were accustomed. Many of the houses on Muncie's Southside that are not abandoned are collapsing, signalling that a way [of] life is disappearing ... People need something to change ... Second, people blame the entire political class for making them desperate. Bringing down trade barriers and letting manufacturing move abroad was part of a western political orthodoxy that became dominant in the 1990s, creating an overcrowded political centre and leaving so much room at the extremes ... Clinton vacillated on it, first backing it, then opposing it. In the wake of Trump's victory Obama has now effectively abandoned TPP, Trump having campaigned heavily against it ... But the issue was not simply about trade or globalisation: to many voters in Muncie, Clinton looked not only like an integral part of the establishment that had brought them to this place, but like a candidate advocating more of the same ... Trump, on the other hand, offered the near certainty that

something would change ... For some who had little to lose, he was evidently a risk worth taking ... Third, and perhaps most dramatic of all, people have come to feel they have no say about what is happening to their lives. That is why the slogan 'Take Back Control' resonated with so many during the Brexit referendum. The nation state is still the primary democratic entity; but given the scale of globalisation it is clearly no longer up to the task of meeting the needs of its citizens. Voters see people coming through borders they can't close and jobs leaving that they can't save and wonder how they can assert themselves on the world. Trump, and his counterparts, are often described in Europe as a threat to democracy. But in truth they would be better understood as the product of a democracy already in crisis".

10   Georg Lukács, *History & Class Consciousness: Studies in Marxist Dialectics*, trans. Rodney Livingstone. Cambridge, Mass.: The MIT Press, 1971, 154.

11   Ibid., 156.

12   Ibid., 158.

13   Ibid., 159.

14   Ibid., 163.

15   Ibid.

16   Ibid., 165.

17   Ibid., 168.

18   Ibid.

19   Ibid.

20   Ibid., 169.

21   Ibid.

22   Ibid., 173.

23   Ibid., 180.

24   Ibid., 181.

25   Ibid., 189.

26   Ibid.

27   Ibid., 193.

28   Ibid., 197.

29   Ibid., 203.
30   Ibid., 204-205.
31   Ibid., 206.

LECTURE FOUR: "UNION POWER AND SOUL POWER"

1   The Congress of Industrial Organizations: a federation of
     trade unions that spanned both the US and Canada.
2   The US election of 1972 took place on 7 November. A few
     months prior, in June, there had been an attempted break-in
     at the Democratic National Committee's headquarters in
     the Watergate office building in Washington, D.C. It later
     emerged, after the election had been won and whilst Nixon
     was in office for his second term, that Nixon himself had
     authorised and funded the break-in using funds from his
     re-election campaign. The president resisted the scandal,
     stalling the investigation. It was eventually revealed that he
     had deployed various illegal and clandestine techniques to
     both protect himself and throw investigators of the scent. It
     was not enough. Many witnesses testified against him and so,
     in late 1973, Nixon was impeached for obstruction of justice,
     abuse of power, and contempt of congress. Before there could
     be a trial, Nixon resigned the presidency in August 1974.
3   "Early in the morning of the last day of the 1960s, three
     hired assassins slipped off their shoes and crept into the
     Yablonski home in southwestern Pennsylvania. One of
     the intruders pulled out a handgun and quickly shot the
     Yablonskis' twenty-five-year-old daughter Charlotte while
     she slept. The two others burst into the master bedroom and
     shot Margaret and then fired half a dozen bullets into their
     target, dissident mine workers' leader Jock Yablonski ... This
     grisly triple homicide quickly became the talk of the nation
     in the first weeks of 1970, and as news spread through the
     coalfields, twenty thousand coal miners laid down their tools
     and walked off the job to protest the state of their union".

See: Jefferson Cowie, *Stayin' Alive: The 1970s and the Last Days of the Working Class*. New York and London: The New Press, 2010, 23.

4   Fisher's less generalised use of the word "resentment" here harks back, implicitly, to his brief mention of *ressentiment* in the first lecture. See: Lecture One, footnote 31.

5   In her 1989 paper for the *University of Chicago Legal Forum*, "Demarginalizing the Intersection of Race and Sex: A Black Feminist Critique of Antidiscrimination Doctrine, Feminist Theory and Antiracist Politics", Kimberlé Crenshaw begins with a consideration of the "problematic consequence of the tendency to treat race and gender as mutually exclusive categories of experience and analysis." She argues that an overreliance on the distinctions between these categories often leads to an erasure of those who straddle multiple categories of identity at once. This is to say, to use her own example, that any analysis of the experience of Black people often focuses on the experiences of men, erasing the experiences of those people who are Black but also women. It is worth noting, in the context of Fisher's argument, that class does figure in Crenshaw's original analysis. She argues that progressive politics focuses too readily on dominant categories — something Crenshaw has witnessed in her capacity as a lawyer. She writes that, "in race discrimination cases, discrimination tends to be viewed in terms of sex- or class-privileged Blacks; in sex discrimination cases, the focus is on race- and class-privileged women." This is to say that a "focus on the most privileged group members marginalizes those who are multiply-burdened and obscures claims that cannot be understood as resulting from discrete sources of discrimination." Therefore, someone who is rich, male and White will fair much better before the eyes of the law than someone who is poor, female and Black. Whilst we may generalise that this is predominantly an issue of race, it is important to consider how this confluence of disadvantaged

categories of identity further impacts the perception of a case in a court of law. Nevertheless, Fisher's argument still stands. Over the decades since Crenshaw's paper was first published, with class being disarticulated throughout society, it is a category of identification that is now all the more obscured as a far more discrete source of discrimination. Interestingly, we can witness how this same process has been attempted with race, particularly in orbit of Barack Obama's presidency in the United States. Arguments that we live in a "post-race" society, with "I don't see skin colour" a common defence against accusations of racism, echo the "post-class" politics of the New Labour years in Britain. However, as many have since made clear, this disarticulation of race doesn't magically abolish race as a category, it simply obscures discrimination behind the oppressive naivety of more privileged groups.

6   See: Joan Williams, "What So Many People Don't Get About the U.S. Working Class", *Harvard Business Review*, 10 November 2016: ‹https://hbr.org/2016/11/what-so-many-people-dont-get-about-the-u-s-working-class›

7   "In the era of Donald Trump and Brexit, Oxford Dictionaries has declared "post-truth" to be its international word of the year. Defined by the dictionary as an adjective "relating to or denoting circumstances in which objective facts are less influential in shaping public opinion than appeals to emotion and personal belief", editors said that use of the term "post-truth" had increased by around 2,000% in 2016 compared to last year. The spike in usage, it said, is "in the context of the EU referendum in the United Kingdom and the presidential election in the United States"." See: Alison Flood, "'Post-truth' named word of the year by Oxford Dictionaries", *The Guardian*, 15 November 2016: ‹https://www.theguardian.com/books/2016/nov/15/post-truth-named-word-of-the-year-by-oxford-dictionaries›

8   Cowie, *Stayin' Alive*, 71–72.

9 This is most likely a reference to Trump's assertion that then-leader of the UK Independence Party (UKIP) Nigel Farage would be the perfect ambassador and go-between for the UK government and Trump's emerging administration. See: Nicky Woolf and Jessica Elgot, "Nigel Farage Would be Great UK Ambassador to US, Says Donald Trump", *The Guardian*, 22 November 2016: <https://www.theguardian.com/politics/2016/nov/22/nigel-farage-uk-ambassador-us-donald-trump>

10 See: Christopher Lasch, *The Culture of Narcissism: American Life in an Age of Diminishing Expectations*. New York: W.W. Norton & Company, 1979.

11 Cowie, *Stayin' Alive*, 73.

12 In the context of the UK high street, this is likely a reference to the nationwide chain of "cocktail bars, restaurant and party venues" known as Revolution. See: <https://www.revolution-bars.co.uk/>

Lecture Five: Libidinal Marxism

1 Jean-François Lyotard, *Libidinal Economy*, trans. Iain Hamilton Grant. London and New York: Bloomsbury Academic, 2015, 123–124.

2 See: Marcel Mauss, *The Gift: Forms and Functions of Exchange in Archaic Societies*, trans. Ian Cunnison. Eastford, CT.: Martino Fine Books, 2011.

3 Lyotard, *Libidinal Economy*, 121.

4 Ibid., 120.

5 Ibid., xvii.

6 Ibid., xvii-xviii.

7 Ibid., 112.

8 Marx was only able to complete one volume of his monstrous critique of political economy, *Das Kapital*, before his death in 1883. The second and third volumes were edited and completed by his friend and collaborator Friedrich Engels

and published posthumously. A fourth volume was similarly unfinished and has had a far more potted publication history. It was partially published in English in 1952 under the title *A History of Economic Theories*. Furthermore, there is the collection of texts and fragments known as the *Grundrisse* — selections from Marx's notebooks which were not intended for publication but were nonetheless very influential following their eventual publication, particularly in English, in 1973.

9   These two paragraphs are knotted and unclear. For clarity, we might say that Lyotard's perspective is cosmic as opposed to "theatrical". The whole world is not a stage, in this sense — that is, a plane, on top of which actors come, play their part, and then shuffle off to some unseen "backstage" or outside. Lyotard's philosophy concerns a sprawling, formless universe in which there are only bodies and affects and intensities. It is an inhuman vision of capitalism, in this sense, akin to Georges Bataille's theory of a cosmic "general economy" of nature in its totality, instead of a "restricted economy" that is concerned only with the economic currents of capitalism.

10 Lyotard, *Libidinal Economy*, 120.

11 Ibid., 158–159.

12 Ibid., 134.

13 Ibid.

14 To return to Fisher's own analogy of temperature, we cannot understand a measurement of 100°C as being worth 100 "heats". Heat is not, in itself, a quantity but a quality. The number "100" refers to a degree of intensity measured upwards from zero. Nevertheless, as Fisher goes onto discuss, through some quotations from the text, this kind of intensive quantity has a relationship to other kinds of quantity. It is clear, for instance, that an intensive quantity of heat can be directly associated with the actual numerical quantity of, say, radiators. Five radiators will produce more heat than one. For Deleuze and Guattari's discussion of "intensive quantities",

see: Deleuze and Guattari, *Anti-Oedipus*, 30.

15   Lyotard, *Libidinal Economy*, 125.

16   Ibid., 127.

17   Ibid., 128.

18   This confluence of the writings of Karl Marx and the Marquis de Sade is an argument that Lyotard arguably takes up from the likes of Pierre Klossowski, Georges Bataille and Jacques Lacan. It was also a confluence notably taken up by Fisher's lecturer Nick Land (albeit indirectly) in a number of his Nineties essays. See: Pierre Klossowki, *Living Currency*, trans. Daniel W. Smith, Vernon W. Cisney, and Nicolae Morar. London: Bloomsbury Academic, 2017. See also: Nick Land, "Kant, Capital and the Prohibition of Incest: A Polemical Introduction to the Configuration of Philosophy and Modernity" in *Fanged Noumena*.

19   Lyotard, *Libidinal Economy*, 253–273.

20   Deleuze's concept of "the fold" is central to much of his oeuvre. Inspired by the concept of the "monad", taken from the philosophy of Gottfried Wilhelm Leibniz (1646–1716), it is a way of thinking and reducing complex beings into simple substances. Whilst a true definition of the "monad" remains contentious — Leibniz's usage of the concept changed over time — it was, in its final form, Leibniz's term for a substance — or substantial form — that contains a "soul" or life force. This life force is unknowable but, viewed in light of the concerns of modern philosophy, we might describe it as a kind of unconscious "drive" that straddles the biological / mechanical distinction explored by Fisher in Lecture Two. What is perhaps even more important, however, is just not what a monad *is* but how we might go about describing its geometry. Deleuze's use of the term "fold" is one such attempt to describe this geometry. It is less like the folding of a piece of paper and more like the fold made when making bread. The relationship of experience to the becoming of subjectivity, in this regard, is like the kneading of raisins into

dough. To speak of these raisins is to speak of an inside from outside. This is similarly how we speak of subjective experiences; as the inside of the outside. It is also worth noting that the example of baking bread is not simply an analogy but an equally valid example of this process. For Deleuze, it allows for us to think not only the production of human subjectivity but non-human subjectivity also. This is important for Fisher as it is a process explored implicitly in his final book *The Weird and the Eerie* — a usage that it is somewhat surprising he does not mention here in his response — in which he speaks to weird and eerie fictions that demonstrate how "the inside is a folding of the outside." For more on Leibnizian monads, see: Lloyd Strickland, *Leibniz's Monadology: A New Translation and Guide*. Edinburgh: Edinburgh University Press, 2014. For more on Deleuze's concept of the fold, see: Gilles Deleuze, *The Fold: Leibniz and the Baroque*, trans. Tom Conley. Minneapolis: University of Minnesota Press, 1992; Gilles Deleuze, *Foucault*, trans. Seán Hand. London: Bloomsbury; Continuum, reprint edition, 2006. For Mark Fisher's invocation of the function of the fold, see: Mark Fisher, *The Weird and the Eerie*. London: Repeater Books, 2016, 11-12.

APPENDIX ONE: COURSE SYLLABUS

1   For more information on this series of events, visit: <https://postcapitalistdesire.wordpress.com/>

APPENDIX TWO: "NO MORE MISERABLE MONDAY MORNINGS" TRACKLIST

1   Mark Fisher, "No more miserable Monday mornings", *k-punk*, 18 July 2015: <https://k-punk.org/no-more-miserable-monday-mornings/>

Repeater Books

is dedicated to the creation of a new reality. The landscape of twenty-first-century arts and letters is faded and inert, riven by fashionable cynicism, egotistical self-reference and a nostalgia for the recent past. Repeater intends to add its voice to those movements that wish to enter history and assert control over its currents, gathering together scattered and isolated voices with those who have already called for an escape from Capitalist Realism. Our desire is to publish in every sphere and genre, combining vigorous dissent and a pragmatic willingness to succeed where messianic abstraction and quiescent co-option have stalled: abstention is not an option: we are alive and we don't agree.